THE
ECONOMIC APPRAISAL
OF ENVIRONMENTAL
PROJECTS AND POLICIES

A Practical Guide

ORGANISATION FOR ECONOMIC CO-OPERATION AND DEVELOPMENT

ORGANISATION FOR ECONOMIC CO-OPERATION AND DEVELOPMENT

Pursuant to Article 1 of the Convention signed in Paris on 14th December 1960, and which came into force on 30th September 1961, the Organisation for Economic Co-operation and Development (OECD) shall promote policies designed:

- to achieve the highest sustainable economic growth and employment and a rising standard of living in Member countries, while maintaining financial stability, and thus to contribute to the development of the world economy;
- to contribute to sound economic expansion in Member as well as non-member countries in the process of economic development; and
- to contribute to the expansion of world trade on a multilateral, non-discriminatory basis in accordance with international obligations.

The original Member countries of the OECD are Austria, Belgium, Canada, Denmark, France, Germany, Greece, Iceland, Ireland, Italy, Luxembourg, the Netherlands, Norway, Portugal, Spain, Sweden, Switzerland, Turkey, the United Kingdom and the United States. The following countries became Members subsequently through accession at the dates indicated hereafter: Japan (28th April 1964), Finland (28th January 1969), Australia (7th June 1971), New Zealand (29th May 1973), Mexico (18th May 1994), the Czech Republic (21st December 1995), Hungary (7th May 1996), Poland (22nd November 1996) and Korea (12th December 1996). The Commission of the European Communities takes part in the work of the OECD (Article 13 of the OECD Convention).

Publié en français sous le titre :

ÉVALUATION ÉCONOMIQUE DES POLITIQUES ET PROJETS ENVIRONNEMENTAUX
UN GUIDE PRATIQUE

Reprinted 2000

FOREWORD

It is now widely recognised that the path to sustainable development involves a better integration of economics into environmental decision-making, in particular through the use of economic techniques for the appraisal of projects and policies. This is why the OECD decided to elaborate manuals for the application of economic valuation techniques for the use of both industrialised and developing countries.

In 1994, a comprehensive technical manual was published *"Project and Policy Appraisal: Integrating Economics and the Environment"*, OECD, Paris. The objective of the present Manual is to provide a simplified whilst comprehensive overview of economic valuation techniques. It is aimed at giving to the non specialist a practical guide to explaining the fundamentals, strengths and weaknesses, fields of applications and sources of information. It must be seen as a complement to the previous more technical manual. It has been prepared with reference to both industrialised and developing countries situations.

This manual has been written by Mr. James Winpenny (Overseas Development Institute, London). The structure of the manual was discussed by the OECD Group on Economic and Environment Policy Integration and a group of experts from both industrialised and developing countries at a joint OECD-EDI workshop in Paris in July 1994. We wish to acknowledge the contribution of the workshop participants and the assistance of both ODI (London) and of the Economic Development Institute from the World Bank (EDI, Washington, DC).

FOREWORD

TABLE OF CONTENTS

Chapter 4
SOURCES OF INFORMATION

Chapter 5
THE MARKET VALUATION OF PHYSICAL EFFECTS

Chapter 6
SURVEY METHODS: CONTINGENT VALUATION

Chapter 7

REVEALED PREFERENCES AND PROXY MARKETS

Chapter 8

DEALING WITH TIME

Chapter

RISK AND UNCERTAINTY

Chapter 10
ENVIRONMENTAL PRICING

Appendix
A SHORT BIBLIOGRAPHY

PREFACE

How to Use the Manual

The **target reader** of the Manual is someone:
- with some economic understanding, though not necessarily a professional economist;
- whose duties include advising and/or taking decisions on environmental policy;
- requiring an understanding of how environmental effects can be valued in economic terms, and why it is important to do so;
- involved in commissioning, interpreting and presenting the results of valuation studies;
- interested primarily in developing and emerging countries (though the Manual has potential relevance to all situations);
- based in either the private or public sectors.

The **layout** of the Manual can be understood through expressing a series of questions that are likely to be raised by the typical reader:

Am I an economist?
Economists may wish to omit the first two chapters and proceed directly to Chapter 3.

Do I need to understand, or explain, why environmental economics is useful and necessary?
Chapters 1 and 2 provide background which should be helpful to both non-economists and to general economists without a specific background in the environment.

What are the environmental problems to be addressed, and what valuation methods are appropriate?
Chapter 3 is an introduction to the valuation methods available, and provides guidance on which of them are appropriate to specific environmental problems.
Chapter 4 should also be read, since the type of information available, or readily accessible, also affects the choice of valuation technique.

How do I go about assembling information for the analysis?

Chapter 4 reviews the main types of information commonly used in environmental analysis. It provides guidance on the question of how much information to collect, and how much should be spent on data assembly. Chapter 5, 6 and 7 provide more detail on the kind of information required by specific valuation methods.

How is valuation actually done?

Depending on which method is selected, chapters 5, 6 and 7 should be consulted. These chapters are written for readers who have to commission such work, or interpret and present the results of valuation studies. They also provide guidance to readers charged with actually undertaking valuation studies. However, some such studies do require specialist knowledge, and the chapters contain suggestions for further reading.

What are the main problems that will arise?

Each of Chapters 5, 6 and 7 contain a section discussing the most common problems or limitations of the methods described. In addition, Chapter 8 discusses how to deal with the controversial question of time and discounting, while Chapter 9 provides guidance on the treatment of risk and uncertainty.

What next? What is the relevance of environmental valuation to policies and prices in the real world?

Chapter 10, dealing with environmental pricing, discusses how the values generated in the process of appraisal can be incorporated into actual prices. The role of prices are considered in the context of all the other instruments of environmental policy.

Chapter 1

INTRODUCTION: WHY THIS PRACTICAL GUIDE IS NECESSARY

Economics is important for people making decisions affecting our environment. The environment will continue to suffer unless economists become more fully involved in analysis and policy-making. That is the principal message of this Manual.

Unless the real costs and benefits of projects, including their impact on the environment, are fully accounted for, bad projects will be chosen, and good projects will not get a fair consideration. If environmental damage and depletion is not entered into national income accounts, governments, their citizens, and international agencies receive the wrong signals about an economy's true performance.

The Manual's target readership, as defined in the Preface, can be broadly divided into two types: **sceptics** who doubt that economics has much to contribute, and need to be persuaded otherwise; and **believers** who accept the principles of environmental economics but need guidance on how it can be applied in practice. There are also many **potential believers** who are still sceptical about the robustness and applicability of the methods involved.

Economists are committed to the principle that economic efficiency should be a fundamental criterion of public investment and policy-making. This implies that scarce resources should be used to maximise the benefits from them, net of the costs of using them in each case. This principle is now enshrined in the widespread use of cost-benefit analysis (CBA) as a decision tool (see Chapter 2). CBA is merely a method of judging projects and policy proposals according to the size of their net economic benefits.

A generation ago, the OECD pioneered the development of a methodology for the application of **social** cost-benefit analysis to the appraisal of development projects (Little and Mirrlees, 1969). This methodology was based on financial appraisal techniques long used in the private sector, adapted and extended for use in public sector decision-making. The current initiative, represented by this Field Manual and its companion Technical Volume (OECD 1994) aims to take this process of methodological adaptation further, by incorporating environmental factors into basic CBA.

The Manual's aim is not to supplant the criterion of economic efficiency but to incorporate environmental factors into it. There is no need for a separate "environmental" criterion if environmental effects can be valued in economic terms. If that is the case, using a modified economic criterion would suffice.

The fundamental assertion of this Manual is that many environmental effects can be subject to economic valuation for appraisal purposes. This is not to argue that the manifold values of the environment can be reduced to economic coinage; this is evidently not true. However, it is often illuminating to illustrate the economic impact of environmental change, which valuation can do. More broadly, much environmental harm is due to economic causes and an understanding of these factors is a precondition of environmental policy formation.

The Manual is about **policy** as well as **projects**. Environmental economics is concerned with the economic motives, amongst others, which underlie the degradation of our habitats. The injection of economics into environmental policy reform involves modifying or working with private incentives, within a suitable legal and institutional framework.

This chapter establishes the rationale for environmental economic valuation and policy-making. Economists explain environmental degradation in terms of **market and policy failure**. These basic concepts are explained below.

1.1. Market Failures

A successful economy depends on a well-functioning market, which signals the relative scarcity of different resources through their prices, and allocates them to their most highly valued uses.

If too much of the environment is being "consumed" (*e.g.* too many trees cut down, too many fish caught, too much effluent poured into rivers) this is a sign that the market is failing to signal the growing scarcity of environmental resources (forests, fisheries, the capacity of rivers to assimilate waste). Looked at from the supply side, the same failure is evident. People are not investing in the environment (planting trees, conserving wildlife, cleaning up rivers) because it is not advantageous for them as individuals to do so. For various reasons, the market is not rewarding environmental conservers and investors (Box 1.1).

Market failure has a number of elements. Eight of these are discussed in Box 1.1. Some of these apply to other sectors of the economy, but they arise with particular severity in the case of natural resources.

Box 1.1.   **Market failure and the environment**

Much of the mismanagement and inefficient use of natural resources and the environment can be traced to malfunctioning, distorted or totally absent markets. Prices generated by such markets do not reflect the true social costs and benefits of resource use. Such prices convey misleading information about resource scarcity and provide inadequate incentives for management, efficient use, and conservation of natural resources. (Panayotou, 1993, p. 33).

Sources of market failure

- Externalities.
- Unpriced assets and missing markets.
- Public goods.
- Transactions costs.
- Property rights.
- Ignorance and uncertainty.
- Short-sightedness.
- Irreversibility.

Source: From Panayotou, 1993.

Externalities are the effects of an action on other parties which were not taken into account by the perpetrator. A firm releasing effluent into a river used for bathing and drinking is causing externalities, which reduce the welfare or increase the costs of other people. These repercussions do not enter into the private calculations of the firm. In other words, the market does not signal the cost of externalities back to the perpetrator, who has no incentive to curb this anti-social behaviour (unless, of course, there are regulations and fines governing such actions). Externalities can also be beneficial, *e.g.* the value of trees, planted for their timber value, as a windbreak for adjacent farmers.

Externalities are all-pervasive. They occur whenever an individual or firm can get away with anti-social behaviour without incurring sanctions. The task of policy makers, where it is feasible, is to **internalise** externalities, by imposing on offenders themselves the full costs of their actions on others (see Chapter 10).

Another cause of market failure is the fact that many **environmental assets are unpriced,** and as a result cannot be traded in a market. There is a **missing market** for environmental quality. Assets prized by society, such as clean air, attractive landscapes and the diversity of biological resources, are not bought and sold in markets. Unless restrained by other measures, individuals have no incentive to reduce their use of these assets, still less invest in their preservation and growth. Many goods and services obtained from nature are available to users at little or no cost apart from that of collection (*e.g.* firewood cut from public forests, fish caught in the sea, wild game hunted).

In some cases, resources are unpriced because they are **public goods**, and charging for them would be difficult or impossible. A public good is one that is available to everyone and which cannot be denied to anyone. As a consequence, it is impossible to charge for its use. It is therefore unprofitable for a private party to invest in its protection or enhancement – because of the impossibility of recovering costs from users (**free riders**). There is also no incentive for a user to abstain from consumption – since someone else would step in instead. This quality of public goods is called **non-exclusivity**.

Some public goods can be enjoyed by a particular user without reducing their supply to others (*e.g.* the existence of biodiversity, preservation of rare species, enjoyment of clean air and water, attractive scenery, the protection of a watershed). Other public goods, while possessing non-exclusivity, are depletable – when one person's use is at the expense of someone else's (*e.g.* use of a public forest for firewood and timber, hunting wild game, sea fishing, use of irrigation water, grazing animals on common pastures).

Some of the worst environmental degradation occurs in resources which are depletable but, in practice (if not in theory), non-excludable. The herder who lets his/her animals onto a public grazing area is imposing costs on other herders (less grass) but in many circumstances it is difficult to exclude a particular user. No-one, except the government or community as a whole, has an incentive to invest in conserving or improving that pasture. Even worse, no individual herder has any (market) incentive to reduce his/her use of the pasture, since any benefit would soon be negated by someone else's use. This situation has been called the **Tragedy of the Commons** (it applies to situations of open access to resources, and may exaggerate the problem in other cases where there are effective systems – often traditional – of common property management).

Implicit in the Tragedy of the Commons is the assumption that the users of the common resource (the pasture) are unable or unwilling to get together to agree a viable system of management. Although each of them has a cogent short term interest in maximising their use of the common resource, in the long term each of them has a stronger incentive to preserve it even if that means accepting limitations on access. There are many reasons, however, why the parties fail to reach agreement – the cost and difficulty of enforcing contracts and policing a deal, the time and trouble of getting many parties together, the cost of supplying information, etc. Collectively these costs are known as **transactions costs**. Where they are high relative to the benefits which are expected, effective agreement is unlikely and the environment continues to be degraded.

Markets, to perform well, need to be supported by institutions and, specifically, a system of **property rights**. An obvious case is the farmer: someone who owns his/her land has an obvious incentive to look after it and reinvest in it, especially if it is also possible to sell it and realise those investments. The same is true of someone with a long and secure lease on land. Tenant farmers, squatters, and those enjoying only the right to use land (usufruct) have much less incentive to manage their land or invest in it, and indeed have every reason to squeeze as much as possible from the soil while they still occupy it. This is not necessarily an argument for the extension of freehold tenure, but for clarifying farmers' legal position and protecting and rewarding careful land management.

Property rights do not only concern land. Water laws in many countries confer the right to use water passing over one's property, or found underneath it: in many places these rights can be bought and sold in active markets. So long as property rights, in their general sense, are clear, exclusive, secure, enforceable and transferable, their owners have every incentive to safeguard their resource. If some or all of these conditions are absent this incentive is diminished.

In developing countries much environmental degradation follows from the attempt by the modern state to override customary laws, or to nationalise resources (forests, common land) which was formerly subject to local customary management. In practice these actions often sow confusion and uncertainty, the traditional system of control is undermined, without being replaced by an effective alternative.

Ignorance and uncertainty also hinder the functioning of markets. The function of markets is to signal emerging scarcities, such as environmental resources. The problem arises because environmental processes are badly understood, and changes (and their implications) may not be perceived in time for prices to operate. Even well-intentioned firms and individuals are unlikely to adjust their behaviour if they, and society, are ignorant about the results of their activities, which may arise over a long period, or at a point remote from themselves.

Short-sightedness (myopia) compounds the problem. Most individuals have quite short planning horizons, in the sense that they pay greatest attention to financial and welfare considerations occurring in the near future. The fact that planting trees may yield great benefits after 30 years, or that nuclear power poses huge costs of de-commissioning and materials disposal after 80-100 years does not weigh very heavily in most people's decisions. Firms commonly expect investments to pay back their outlay in 5-7 years. Governments are supposed to be able to take a longer view on behalf of their constituents, but electoral considerations often dictate otherwise. The result of collective myopia is that both long term costs and benefits tend to be heavily discounted when decisions are made. Environmental projects are particularly liable to this bias.

Finally, markets fail when environmental processes are **irreversible**. Where the future is uncertain, there is value in keeping future development options open. Where an attractive valley is flooded to create a hydro-electric scheme, society loses the option of preserving that landscape for future generations. Generating the same power from a thermal power station would retain that option, yet the market would point to the hydro project if it were cheaper. In other words, the market would ignore the option values which are destroyed by building the dam. This issue is an important one in practice because society is becoming increasingly interested in environmental quality, which means that option values are rising all the time.

It follows that a central part of any government's environmental policy should be redressing the above market failures. This calls for an active agenda: it is decidedly not a prescription for *laisser-faire*, or letting prices find a natural level. For instance, if externalities are to be identified and "internalised" in some way, financial transfers have to be arranged between the perpetrator and "victim". Chapter 10 reverts to these, and other, aspects of environmental policy-making.

The other major cause of environmental damage is **policy failure**. The above catalogue of market failures does not imply that the environment is safe in the hands of policy-makers. Governments have shown themselves to be imperfect guardians of the national interest, and have often intervened in markets to make situations worse. The term policy failure covers both omissions and commissions – not only a failure to correct market distortions and biases, but also the introduction of new distortions or a worsening of existing ones. A few examples can be given (Box 1.2).

Box 1.2.   **Examples of policy failure**

- Low prices of irrigation water.
- Subsidised prices for energy.
- Pesticide subsidies.
- Tax incentives and credit subsidies for ranching.
- Bureaucratic obstacles to land titling.
- Half-baked land reforms creating tenure insecurity.
- Low logging royalties.
- Nationalisation of forests, without means to control and manage.

Sizeable parts of important irrigation systems (*e.g.* the Indus Valley) are becoming saline and waterlogged, reducing their fertility, because too much water is applied and drainage is poor. Reasons vary, but in some cases this is due to the public good nature of irrigation water (specifically, its non-exclusivity) which leads to over-consumption. In many instances it is due to the failure to include drainage when the schemes were designed. But the situation is made worse by the universal failure of irrigation agencies to charge a price for their water which is anywhere near the cost of supplying it, hence farmers have little incentive to use it sparingly.

In many countries, including economies in transition, the use of energy (coal, oil, electricity) is highly subsidised. Domestic, industrial and government consumers have acquired profligate and wasteful habits of energy use. This not only causes faster depletion of their coal, oil and hydro potential, storing up future supply problems, but also causes serious air pollution. The grave traffic congestion in cities such as Lagos, Manila and Bangkok is also a sign that the costs to motorists of entering central areas is less than the extra cost they impose on other motorists, and on society from the congestion and pollution they cause. Higher fuel costs are an obvious part of any policy package to relieve the situation.

The destruction of Amazonian forest in the late 1970s and 1980s was fuelled by comprehensive policy distortions. The tax-exempt status of agriculture, supplemented by special tax credit for large ranches, led to a rush to acquire land, which was converted for livestock. Smaller settlers came in behind the ranchers, and their award of title depended on evidence of deforestation. Credit was available at very low interest rates, and was widely used by ranchers. Without the various kinds of subsidy, it is unlikely that ranching would have been profitable, since it was only sustainable for a few years. The subsidies tilted the balance of attractiveness in favour of (unsustainable) farming, compared to the preservation, or sustainable management, of the natural forest.

1.2. Sustainable Development (SD)

Much environmental discussion centres on the concept of SD. It is not enough for a project to perform well on the normal financial and economic criteria. If it makes substantial use of natural resources, or environmental "sink" functions (such as the capacity of air and water for waste assimilation), a project may be profitable on conventional criteria yet non-sustainable in environmental terms. Keeping options open for future generations, which is one accepted definition of SD, is a good idea, but is too vague for operational purposes.

Many economists view the environment as a form of natural capital, analogous in some ways to physical or financial capital assets. Damaging the environment is therefore similar to running down capital, which sooner or later reduces the value of its recurrent services (or income stream). Some level of environmental use is in some sense "sustainable" and consistent with preserving environmental capital.

SD should leave our total patrimony, including natural environmental assets, intact over time. We should bequeath to future generations the same "capital", embodying opportunities for potential welfare, that we currently enjoy.

The literal view of the environment as a capital stock that should not be diminished is difficult to interpret and apply. But its value is in reminding us that human activities consume various kinds of environmental resources, which need to be restored in the long term unless we are all to become poorer. Certain kinds of environmental asset can be restored relatively easily, others not at all.

Environmental economics distinguishes three broad types of capital. **Man-made capital** (factories, roads, houses, etc.) can be increased or decreased at our discretion (ignoring, for the moment, the sacrifices and demands on the natural environment that are entailed). **Critical natural capital** (ozone layer, global climate, biodiversity, wildernesses, Antarctica, etc.) comprises natural assets essential to life that cannot be replaced or substituted by man-made capital. The third category – **other natural capital** – includes renewable natural resources and some finite mineral resources that can be wholly or partly replenished or substituted by man-made capital.

Some kinds of natural capital are vital, irreplaceable, and beyond price. The preservation of such assets should be an absolute constraint on all activities: it implies setting safe minimum standards (*e.g.* for water and air quality, preservation of biodiversity) and ruling certain kinds of development out of bounds.

Other types of non-critical natural capital should if possible be valued using the methods discussed in this Manual. If activities lead to a reduction in natural capital (by using up resources in production, or destroying them through pollution or other externalities), these "costs" should be measured, and debited to the activity responsible for them. They can either remain notional (shadow) values used only for planning and appraisal, or they can be made actual charges to the project (*e.g.* by building in compensation from gainers to losers, or insisting on specific environmental protection measures).

The use of finite resources (*e.g.* minerals and fossil fuels) is non-sustainable in the strict sense. Advocates of SD acknowledge that finite resources often need to be used up in development, but urge that research should take place into alternatives and substitutes, that efficiency in their use should be improved, that part of their revenues should be used to create a capital fund to sustain income, etc.

The principles of SD can be applied to project analysis by using the **sustainability criterion** (Box 1.3).

Box 1.3.   **The Sustainability Criterion**

Sustainable projects should observe the following criteria:
- place economic values on environmental costs and benefits;
- avoid damage to critical natural capital so far as possible;
- avoid irreversible processes;
- limit the use of renewable natural assets to their sustainable yield; otherwise, including the costs of replacing these assets, *e.g.* through a "compensatory" project;
- use appraisal values to determine "green" prices for use in the real world.

1.3. The Relevance of Environmental Valuation

The valuation methods that are discussed from Chapter 3 onwards help the cause of SD in several ways:

- providing a truer account of the real costs and benefits of projects and policies by quantifying their environmental effects. This helps to offset some of the market failures noted earlier, penalises schemes with environmental costs, and helps to promote those with environmental benefits;

- furnishing the raw data for national resource accounting, which adjusts national accounts (GNP, GDP, etc.) to allow for environmental "depreciation" (soil erosion, depletion of petroleum reserves, deforestation, etc.). These adjustments provide a more accurate indicator of a country's development performance (Box 1.4);

- providing help to environmental policy through "green" pricing. By indicating the size of environmental costs and benefits, valuation provides guidance on the size of taxes, subsidies, user charges and other financial devices necessary to correct market and policy failures.

Box 1.4.   **Environmental costs of agriculture in South Africa**

	$ mn
Gross Domestic Agricultural Product	4 310
Net National Agricultural Income (After wages, salaries and depreciation of reproducible capital)	1 789
Annual Depreciation of Arable Land Resources through:	
• water erosion	26
• wind erosion	2
• soil crusting	9
• soil compaction	8
• increased acidity	27
• salinisation and water logging	10
Annual Depreciation of Arable Land	85
Annual Depreciation of Rangeland	39
Total annual resource depreciation	**124**
Off Farm Costs:	
• Sedimentation of dams	33
• Increased costs of purification	66
Total costs	**224**
Modified net national farm income	**1 565**

Source: Mackenzie, 1994.

Further References and Sources

A very readable and stimulating introduction to environmental policy is contained in Theodore Panayotou, *Green markets*, Harvard Institute for International Development/International Center for Economic Growth and published by the Institute for Contemporary Studies, California, 1993.

Another account with wide popular appeal is Pearce, D., Markandya, A. and Barbier, E., *Blueprint for a green economy*, Earthscan, London, 1989.

Oates, Wallace E. and Cropper, Maureen L., "Environmental economics: a survey", *Journal of Economic Literature*, XXX, June 1992, is a concise and authoritative review.

In French language, see also Barde, J.-Ph., *Économie et politique de l'environnement*, Presses Universitaires de France, Paris, 1992.

The origin of Box 1.4 is a paper by Craig Mackenzie, "Degradation of arable land resources: policy options and considerations within the context of rural restructuring in South Africa". *Land and Agriculture Policy Centre, Policy Paper* No. 11, Johannesburg, December 1994.

The early OECD work on social cost-benefit analysis appeared in two books by I.M.D. Little and J.A. Mirrlees, namely: *Manual of industrial project analysis in developing countries*, 2 volumes, OECD, Paris, 1969, and *Project appraisal and planning for developing countries*, Heinemann, London, 1974.

Chapter 2

ECONOMICS AND THE ENVIRONMENT

Chapter I argued for the usefulness of economic valuation in our dealings with environmental matters. The purpose of this chapter is to explain some of the basic principles that determine economic values. It will introduce the reader to the main concepts of economic value, how they are incorporated into standard project analysis, and how the "economistic" approach fits in with other decision-making frameworks.

2.1. Economic Concepts of "Value"

To the economist, scarcity is what imparts value to a good or service. Something that is abundantly available to all who wish to consume it has no economic value, however much it may be desirable on moral, aesthetic, or other grounds. A beautiful sunset, or clean air, has no **economic** value so long as it is freely available to all. The moment it ceases to be freely available, it has potential economic value.

If the sunset is spoiled by air pollution, or by building developments on the skyline, or if clean air become polluted, these assets start to become scarce. People will start to reveal, by their decisions to locate, or in their spending plans, their **preferences** for environmental quality. In this case, "environmental quality" is akin to a good which is becoming scarce. Its value can be inferred from what people would be willing to pay to improve or restore it, or to protect themselves against a further decline, using the various techniques discussed in the following chapters.

Where a market for the good or service exists, its scarcity is measured by its price. As discussed in Chapter I, there are many kinds of market failures. For many types of environmental "goods" (*e.g.* the sunset example) there are simply no markets, and economists have to resort to other valuation methods. For other environmental assets, the market price fails for various reasons to signal their true scarcity. However, where markets operate reasonably well, prices will give a reliable indication of a good's relative scarcity. As Chapters 5 to 7 will indicate, markets can provide direct or indirect evidence of the scarcity of many environmental assets.

23

A market is where the supply of a product or service confronts the demand for it. The normal economic assumption, borne out by much empirical evidence, is that the higher the price, the more of a good is supplied and the less is demanded, and vice versa. The relationship between supply, demand and price can be depicted by a figure as in Box 2.1 with the point of intersection denoting where the price of the good tends to be fixed.

Just as the price influences the amounts supplied and demanded, so a change in supply or demand can feed back to price. For instance, the fall in the demand for ivory following the CITES ban on ivory trading has led to a fall in its price. On the other hand, the selective cutting of valuable tropical hardwoods, without replanting, is likely to cause a secular increase in their price on world markets.

However, prices determined in this way are likely to give only a **minimum** estimate of values. In Box 2.1 the total satisfaction of the consumer is represented by the entire area under the demand curve. The area D–P1–P which lies above the price actually paid is the **consumers surplus**, indicating the excess of what the consumer would have been willing to pay over what he or she actually had to pay.

The consumers surplus should be added to benefits whenever the demand curve is downward sloping, as in Box 2.1. The concept is important for many kinds of environmental assets, the price of which is zero or very small, *e.g.* public beaches, or national parks. It also applies to services where the fee charged is much below what users would be willing to pay, *e.g.* concession fees and royalties paid by lumber companies to cut forests, or the amounts typically paid by households for their water. In all these cases, taking prices as the measure would seriously underestimate the values of the assets in question.

In short, economic values comprise both the prices paid in markets and the consumer surpluses that users obtain. The latter are derived from a demand curve which measures the user's **willingness to pay (WTP)** for the service, namely how much they would forego in income to obtain an increase in environmental quality. This is an indication of their **preferences**. *The attempt to put economic values on the environment can also be expressed as determining peoples' environmental preferences.*

2.2. Total Economic Value

Where valuing the environment is concerned, market prices have other shortcomings than the ones already discussed. The easiest kinds of environmental benefits to envisage are those accruing to users – people who directly use the asset in question, and who derive **direct use values** from them. Forests and soils are obvious

Box 2.1.   **Supply, demand and price**

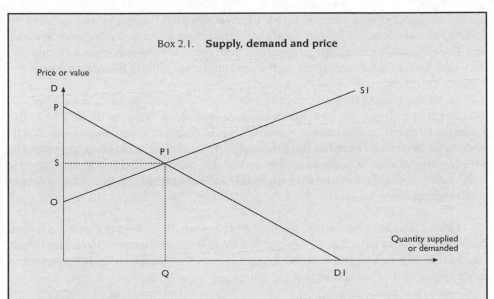

In the diagram, the line D-D1 is the demand curve, indicating what the demand for a good would be (measured along the horizontal axis) at different levels of its price (along the vertical axis). Demand is normally inversely related to price: consumers face income constraints and will reduce their consumption of an item in proportion to the sacrfice in cash that it entails.

S-S1 depicts the supply curve, showing that supply is positively related to price. At a price of P the demand and supply curves intersect and an amount Q is exchanged.

The entire area under the demand curve, D-D1-O measures the potential consumer satisfaction from the good. If the price is fixed at P, the consumer surplus, over and above the price paid, is represented by D-P1-P.

The demand curve D-D1 indicates the consumers' willingness to pay for the good.

The value of a given amount of environmental assets – say the area of land available for hunting and fishing – is given by adding the market value (P x Q) to the consumer surplus (D-P1-P). Because the area D-P1-P is often irregular in practice, due to the non-linear shape of the demand curve at this point, estimation of the consumer surplus will usually have to be done algebraically. Changes in consumers' (and producers') surplus are used to estimate the gross welfare effect. If the change is positive, it counts as a benefit, and if it is negative, a cost.

The marginal cost, or marginal benefit, is the change in total cost or benefit from an increase or decrease in the amount supplied or used. The steeper the supply and demand curves, the higher are marginal costs and benefits.

examples. Another type of value is that of environmental functions, such as soil protection, climatic regulation, and ecological interactions. These are **indirect use values**. Even if people do not currently benefit from the asset either directly or indirectly, they may wish to retain an option on the asset in future. This is the **option value**.

However, people may also value environmental assets even if they do not obtain direct or indirect use from them, or place an option value on them. This is the realm of **bequest** and **existence values**, both examples of non-use values. Existence value is derived from the pure pleasure in something's existence, unrelated to whether the person concerned will ever be able to benefit directly or indirectly from it. Bequest value is similar, though the motive is the desire to pass something on to one's descendants.

The various kinds of values discussed above are illustrated in Box 2.2. Starting from the left hand side, values are highly tangible, and become progressively less so towards the right hand side. This determines the valuation technique that is most appropriate in each case:

- direct use values can be estimated using any of the techniques discussed in this Manual. Compared to other types of values, they are most amenable to market valuation, though the existence of consumer surplus means that the use of prices alone will normally underestimate benefits;

- indirect use values can also be estimated using market-based methods, as well as asking people about their willingness-to-pay;

- option, bequest and existence values can effectively only be discovered from surveys of peoples' preferences, expressed in their willingness-to-pay.

2.3. Cost-Benefit Analysis (CBA)

Whatever values are arrived at in environmental appraisal should be useable in cost-benefit analysis, which is the most common (though not the only) method of project and policy appraisal. Although CBA is most often applied to decisions about **projects**, it is also capable of being used for evaluating **policies**. For instance, in the USA the Safe Drinking Water Act, first passed in 1974, was intended to protect human health by guaranteeing safe public water supplies, but no comparison of its likely benefits and the necessary intake water treatment costs was used in setting the stringent standards. Intake system costs have risen sharply as a result of these standards, and the Environmental Protection Agency estimates that potable water and related sewage costs for the typical household will increase by 50 per cent by 2000 as a result.

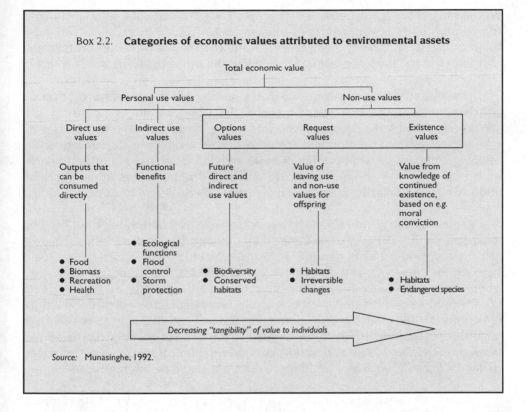

Box 2.2.   **Categories of economic values attributed to environmental assets**

Source: Munasinghe, 1992.

Studies have concluded that the total costs of the water quality program out-weigh the total benefits and that, in many areas, marginal costs exceed marginal benefits. For 1985, annual benefits were estimated at $14 billion with a possible range from $5.7 billion to $27.7 billion, while estimated average annual costs from 1979 to 1988 were $23.2 billion. The benefit estimates, however, fail to include some important values, such as option and existence values, that might increase the benefit-to-cost ratio (Howe, 1991).

CBA is merely a decision tool which judges projects according to a comparison between their costs and benefits. If the proposal shows a net benefit, it can be approved, and different projects can be ranked according to the size of their net benefits. However, the concepts of costs and benefits, and the way they are reckoned in the analysis, need some brief explanation.

There are normally **alternative** ways of achieving the objectives of a project. Sponsors of projects (engineers, doctors, even environmentalists, etc.) usually pretend that there is not, because they are wedded to a particular solution. But it is the responsibility of economists to probe whether all feasible alternatives have been explored, and satisfy themselves that the chosen one is the most robust and cost-effective (*i.e.* the least cost way of fulfilling the project's aims).

These alternatives might include doing nothing, delaying, phasing, or taking policy measures rather than spending decisions. Doing nothing is a perfectly reasonable option in some circumstances, with its own costs and benefits, and is preferable to carrying out a project that wastes resources. In any case, the consequences of doing nothing (the **without-project case**) should be assessed in order to judge what real difference the project would make. The point is important where an underlying trend is taking place, which the project is designed to alleviate.

Resources that go into a project have alternative uses. If they were not used up in a particular project they could be used for other purposes, some of which would also have a positive rate of return. For instance, the land claimed for a factory could be used for housing, or for grazing cattle. Its skilled labour could get work elsewhere. Its unskilled labour may have the choice of going back to work on the land. Locally produced raw cotton used in a textile factory could be exported in unprocessed form. Where such resources (inputs) have alternative uses they can obviously not be regarded as "free" or as uniquely earmarked or destined for the project in hand. Each input has an **opportunity cost**, and should contribute in output to the project at least as much as it could produce in the next best alternative use.

Time is a crucial dimension when assessing projects and in making comparisons between them. One project might have a large flow of benefits almost immediately, but have all its investment cost concentrated in the first year or two (*e.g.* purchase of flue desulphurisation units for power stations). Another project might have long delayed benefits, but have investment costs that are also spread out over a number of years (*e.g.* an afforestation scheme). How can a comparison be made? An equally common problem is to make a comparison between a project with a high initial cost but a low running cost, and an alternative with a lower initial cost but a higher running cost (*e.g.* a hydroelectric power scheme compared with a thermal electric plant). In both cases a true comparison can only be made by allowing for the time factor, tracing the incidence over time of costs and benefits, and using an appraisal method that takes this into account. The concept is to **discount** costs and benefits, further discussion of which is postponed until Chapter 8.

CBA draws a distinction between nominal, or financial, values, and economic ones. A private investor is interested in the actual money costs and returns on his project, and reacts to the net effect on his or her bank balance. A government, however, needs to see through the financial rate of return to perceive the economic costs and benefits to the economy. There are several major differences between the concepts of the **economic and financial rates of return**.

i) Economic costs differ from financial ones. They try to measure the real, or resource, cost to the economy from undertaking a particular activity. Where inputs are subsidised, financial costs will be below economic ones. Where inputs are taxed, financial costs will exceed economic costs. Sometimes the extent of the subsidy or tax is concealed, *e.g.* when an item is supplied by a monopoly or loss-making nationalised industry. Where, because of minimum statutory wages or trade union pressure, wages are set at a certain level, but workers would have been willing to work for less, the financial cost of labour may exceed its economic cost. The economic value of an input is sometimes referred to as its "shadow" (or "accounting") price.

ii) Economic benefits are not the same as financial revenue. This is most obvious where benefits are not fully quantified, *e.g.* in public health or water supply projects, or where they are measurable but do not directly accrue in financial form, *e.g.* road user cost savings. In both cases consumers' surplus may be used to approximate benefits. A difference may also arise where output is sold in a protected market, or conversely where exports are disposed of at an over-valued exchange rate.

iii) A project may give rise to externalities (both costs and benefits) which the private investor can safely ignore.

Where money costs and benefits in an economy are seriously distorted in various ways, a project's inputs and outputs should be valued according to their international or "**border**" **prices**. This entails working out what they would cost if imported or what they would realise if exported.

An important distinction is between **uncertainty** and **risk** (further discussed in Chapter 9). Uncertainty describes ignorance about the future, while risk is the likelihood of specific outcomes occurring. One crude method of allowing for uncertainty is to demand a higher rate of return from the riskier projects (*e.g.* by applying a higher cut-off discount rate). This is analogous to the private entrepreneur who regards profits as the rewards for risk-taking, and requires a higher profit from riskier projects. However, it is more satisfactory to work out the rate of return from the **most probable outcome**. The method is to describe the various possible outcomes (or combinations of events) and to try and attach a probability to each occurring. Each outcome is thus weighted by the probability of it happening, and they can all be added up to produce a central, or most probable, rate of return. However, policy-makers will be interested in knowing the likelihood of the extreme outcomes occurring, especially the chance of complete disaster.

Finally, **sensitivity analysis**, which is further discussed below, tries to pinpoint the events which would have the greatest effect on the outcome of a project. Experience shows that projects usually turn out very differently from what was expected. Sensitivity analysis tests the impact of events and changes that would make or break the project.

Virtually all economic decision rules employ discounting, which enables streams of costs and benefits to be compared on an equal footing allowing for the years in which they occur, and which can reduce both streams to a single figure, namely **present value**. This approach applies equally to economic and financial analysis (the notion of discounted cash flow was first developed for use in private companies).

CBA may be done using three main decision rules. The major difference is between the **internal rate of return** (IRR) criterion and the other two, **net present value** and **benefit-cost ratio** (BCR) (Box 2.3). The IRR is the discount rate at which the streams of costs and benefits are equal.

The higher the IRR, the better the project, so projects with a higher IRR are to be preferred to those with a lower IRR. The IRR method has the convenience that it enables a comparison to be made between the rate of return of projects and the minimum, or cut-off rate, that the government or sponsoring agency may stipulate, and rates of return on other feasible investments. Thus an electricity corporation may be set

Box 2.3.   **NPV, IRR and BCR ($)**

Year	Cost	Benefit	Discounted net benefit (10%)
0	100	—	−100
1	—	30	27
2	—	40	33
3	—	50	38
4	—	50	34
			32

Note: Net present value (NPV) = $32
Internal rate of return (IRR) = 18%
Benefit-cost ratio (BcR) = 1.32:1.0

In this example, an initial investment of $100 yields a return of $30, 40 and 50. The final column shows the net sum of costs and benefits for each year, dicounted at 10%. The sum of the final column is $32, which is the NPV of the investment. The IRR is the discount rate at which the sum of the final column is reduced to zero. This is 18 per cent in the example, which exceeds the discount rate actually used (10%) by a confortable margin.

minimum target rates of return of, say, 10 per cent. The IRR criterion enables it to accept and reject projects that come out, respectively, above and below 10 per cent. The concept is also intuitively attractive to people who think in terms of private rates of profit, even though the two ideas may be different in other important respects.

The IRR can be defined as that discount rate at which the **net present value** of a project is zero. The concepts of the IRR and NPV are thus inseparable. The NPV is simply the difference between the discounted streams of benefits and costs. It is the value, discounted to the present, of doing the project rather than not doing it. Chapter 8 discusses the practical problem of setting an appropriate discount rate.

The **benefit-cost ratio** is the ratio between discounted total benefits and costs. Thus if discounted total benefits are 120 and discounted total costs 100 the benefit-cost ratio is 1.2:1 (and the NPV is 20). This ratio enables a distinction to be made between projects whose NPV is high because it is large, and projects that have a genuinely high rate of return (IRR). The BCR, like the NPV, should never be quoted without stating the discount rate that has been used.

In most cases, the IRR, NPV and BCR will give the same result and will produce the same ranking of projects according to their attractiveness. There will be a few cases where the use of the IRR on the one hand and the NPV and BCR on the other will produce different results, and these oddities have attracted a disproportionate amount of academic controversy. In general, where the government is using some sort of target (minimum, or cut-off) rate of return on capital, maximising NPV should be the criterion, with the BCR as a supplementary check. However, to some people the IRR is more meaningful and in the last resort the decision-maker will choose the most easily comprehensible formula.

CBA converts costs and benefits to a common currency, and the size of the NPV is one possible measure of the project's desirability. An objection is that using the single indicator of NPV conceals the fact that the project may have an impact on many different parties, including losers as well as gainers. Its **distributional** effects should be explicitly analysed.

In theory, if a project has an NPV of $1 000, this means that up to $1 000 is available to compensate those parties likely to lose from the project. The $1 000 measures the **potential** ability of gainers to compensate losers – either directly, or through the intermediary of the state through taxes, cost recovery and subsidies. In practice, such **actual compensation** will rarely take place.

This standard problem in CBA is especially important for environmental appraisal, where uncompensated externalities are likely to be common. It argues for:

- the careful identification of impacts and their incidence on different groups of people (gainers and losers);
- consideration of mitigation measures to ease the impact on injured parties;
- working out financial and institutional mechanisms to facilitate actual transfers to people likely to lose.

Sometimes the losers will be unborn members of future generations. The special problems of dealing with their interests are discussed further in Chapter 8. Another difficult issue is that CBA is conducted from the viewpoint of **human welfare** (it is **anthropomorphic**). Yet environmental issues concern non-human living species too. Many people would argue that these other species have rights (**standing**) in debates about the environment.

It is idle to pretend that economic criteria, enshrined in such techniques as CBA, can take into account non-human interests. All economic approaches either use the evidence of (human) market values, or use other methods for inferring (human) preferences. What CBA can do is:

- identify, so far as is feasible and as knowledge permits, the wider impact of human interventions;
- invoke the Precautionary Principle or a similar safeguard where impacts on the natural order are likely to be sufficiently grave, or irreversible;
- indicate what costs are involved in protecting non-human species, and appraise alternatives which are less threatening to them.

The interests of non-humans can, of course, only be articulated through humans. But if sufficient people feel strongly enough about non-human species rights, their views can be expressed through democratic channels, and can become a counterweight to the use of purely economic approaches.

Cost-effectiveness is a criterion for judging the most efficient way of performing a given task. Whatever other decision rule is applied, the chosen method should normally also be the most efficient, that is, the cheapest, way of meeting the objectives of the project. Where the project has no measurable (quantifiable) benefits, or where an environmental goal has been set by national authorities or in an international agreement, the cost-effectiveness criterion is the main one to apply. It is very simple, consisting of calculating all the costs, both capital and recurrent, of a project, applying the appropriate shadow prices, and discounting the resulting stream to obtain a present value for costs. This procedure is repeated for the main alternative ways of carrying out the project, and the one with the lowest present value is chosen. Note that this criterion assumes that all the alternatives being compared can carry out the project equally well.

If, on the other hand, there are quality differences in the service being supplied the basis of comparison is invalid.

It follows that cost-effectiveness is a valid decision rule for such activities as the supply of drinking water to a group of villages – where the scope and quality of the service to be provided are closely defined. Once can then select the cheapest among the various alternatives as the "correct" solution without any qualms. However, one would hesitate to apply the same procedure in comparing, say, site and service housing schemes with the construction of cheap prefabricated dwellings, since one would not be comparing like with like, and each would claim to be providing distinctive benefits.

2.4. Other Decision-making Methods

Environmental values are likely to be incorporated into decision methods such as CBA and CEA, which are essentially "economistic". The value judgements underlying CBA and CEA are that individual preferences should count, and that preferences should be weighted by the common factor of money. The first assumes "democratic" values, and the second takes for granted that the distribution of income is acceptable, if not ideal.

Despite these assumptions, which will not always apply, CBA and CEA are systematic, widely recognised, and frequently required as part of official procedures. Although no decision method is completely objective and value-free, CBA and CEA are less arbitrary than most alternatives. However, other methods are available, some of which are mentioned below.

Subjective scoring methods. People representing "expert opinion" are invited to score and rank projects on the basis of stated criteria. This is sometimes known as the "Delphi Technique" (overlooking the fact that the Delphic Oracle always gave enigmatic answers). It allows wider, non-quantifiable and more subjective criteria to enter into decisions on projects.

The risk is that the method can become arbitrary, unless the exercise is well controlled. If, for instance, there are a number of criteria, some quantifiable, others not, it is reasonable to canvass various different opinions on how the project has performed on the non-quantifiable criteria – but the relative weights of the different criteria must be agreed from the outset if the exercise is not to become indeterminate.

Impact Evaluation (IE) assesses the effects of an intervention on its surroundings. It is often carried out ex post, when the project has been completed, and when its impacts have become evident. It might cover many aspects, *e.g.* technical, economic, socio-cultural, institutional and environmental. The rise of IE reflects concerns in particular about the distributional impact of aid projects on target groups, especially the poor, women and children, landless, etc. as well as on the physical environment.

Risk-benefit analysis (RBA) focuses on the prevention of events carrying serious risks. It can be viewed as the inversion of normal CBA, because it starts by presuming no action. The cost of inaction is the likelihood of the risk occurring (*e.g.* an explosion at a chemical works). On the other hand, the benefit of inaction is the saving in the cost of preventive measures. If the costs are less than the benefits, no action is justified, and vice versa.

For projects where risk is the paramount consideration RBA is a useful way of bringing out the issues. It does assume that costs (risks) can be fully captured in money values, which is not always the case. Moreover, the use of expected values is unlikely to give due weight to a catastrophic event with only a small probability. Risk and uncertainty are dealt with at greater length in Chapter 9.

Acceptable risk analysis (ARA). The conventional treatment of risk in CBA, further discussed in Chapter 9, uses expected values and sensitivity analysis, assumes that the various possible outcomes can be defined and specified and that the costs and benefits of each possible outcome can be attributed and measured. These conditions do not always hold for environmental risks, many of which are poorly understood.

ARA tackles the question, "How safe is 'safe enough'?" (Fischhoff *et al.*, 1981). It is an eclectic approach, avoiding exclusive reliance on a single formal method of selecting the most acceptable option. In deciding what is acceptable risk, ARA complements formal methods (like CBA) with professional opinion, takes account of the lessons of past experience. ARA denies that there are value-free methods for choosing the most acceptable option, and requires all parties to understand the value assumptions contained in their views. It is argued that in the case of most new and intricate hazards even so-called objective risks have a large judgemental component. (Fischhoff *et al.*, 1981). Moreover, ARA asserts that the expertise necessary for these decisions is scattered throughout society. Expert opinion should be combined with that of people in all walks of life, including the lay public.

Decision analysis (DA) drops the assumption implicit in CBA that decision-makers are risk-neutral, and analyses the effect of risk-averseness. Expected values are weighted by attitudes to risk to become expected utilities. DA proceeds rather like CBA up to the point where outcomes and probabilities have been established.

At that point, it draws up and assesses decision-makers' preferences, judgements and trade-offs, the purpose being to obtain the weights that decision-makers would attach to outcomes carrying different levels of risk.

For instance, the risk-averse decision-maker would prefer an option which avoided the risk of a particularly bad outcome, to one which offered the chance of greater gain as well as greater loss. The preferences of decision-makers may be expressed in "utility weights" for the various outcomes. These could be used to devise formal decision rules, *e.g.* MiniMax (minimise the maximum possible loss). Finally, the expected utility of each possible outcome is obtained by multiplying the probability of its occurrence by its utility. The preferred alternative is that with the highest expected utility.

Multi-criteria analysis (MCA) is the application of more than one criterion to the task of judging performance. The quantifiable economic rate of return would normally be included if it were available, and – depending on the type of project and their relevance – other criteria might be cost per beneficiary, range and scope (number of beneficiaries), distribution of benefits, ease and speed of implementation, replicability, or other systematic judgements made by experts or decision-makers. In practice, MCA is widely used. Although such methods as cost-benefit analysis purport to give a categorical and definitive rule on the acceptability of a project or policy, most decision makers are more comfortable using CBA alongside other criteria and methods, including subjective judgements.

Further References and Sources

The economic principles underlying environmental appraisal and valuation are explored in greater depth and rigour in the OECD's companion volume to this, *Project and policy appraisal: integrating economics and environment* (Paris, 1994), written by Pearce, Whittington, Georgiou and James.

There are many excellent texts on environmental economics, mostly by academic writers. The above-mentioned OECD book contains a full list of relevant works on this subject.

An elementary account of cost-benefit analysis and a detailed discussion of its practical use in a variety of sectors is given in Bridger, G.A. and Winpenny, J.T., *Planning development projects: a practical guide to the choice and appraisal of public sector investments*. Her Majesty's Stationery Office (HMSO), London, 1983.

The full reference for Howe (1991) is: "An evaluation of US air and water policies" by Charles W. Howe, *Environment*, 33/7, September 1991.

The full reference to Fischhoff (1981) is: Baruch Fischhoff *et al.*: *Acceptable risk*, Cambridge University Press, Cambridge, 1981.

Chapter 3

INTRODUCTION TO ENVIRONMENTAL VALUATION METHODS

In Chapter 1, it was demonstrated that many problems are caused by a failure to value environmental resources. The impact of human decisions on the environment often goes unrecorded in private budgets and balance sheets, or in cost-benefit analyses of public decisions. As a result, too many projects are undertaken which cause environmental damage, and too few activities are chosen which produce environmental benefits.

This chapter introduces the main economic techniques for valuing environmental effects. The choice of method should be pragmatic, the result of several successive steps:

- deciding the type of environmental problem to be analysed;
- reviewing which technique is appropriate for that problem;
- considering what information is required about problem A if method B is to be used;
- assessing whether that information is readily available, and at what cost;
- in the light of the answer to the previous question, reconsidering the choice of valuation method.

This chapter deals with the first two points above. Information sources are discussed in Chapter 4, and Chapters 5, 6 and 7 go into further detail on the principal methods of economic environmental valuation.

3.1. Environmental Issues and Problems

Table 3.1 lists the main kinds of environmental issues and problems confronting countries at all stages of development. They are divided for convenience into "green", "brown", and "blue" issues, with a separate category of "global" concerns.

Each country will rank these different issues according to its own order of priority. **High income developed countries** in temperate latitudes are more likely to be concerned with issues like:

- the disposal of solid and hazardous waste;
- groundwater levels and pollution;
- cleaning up former waste dumps and old industrial sites;
- the effect of agro-chemicals on wildlife;
- safe disposal of agricultural waste, especially animal manure;
- the preservation of wildlands, wetlands, unique and unspoilt landscapes;
- overfishing;
- acid rain;
- managing water resources in the face of growing demands;
- conservation of biodiversity and wildlife in other countries;
- global warming and the ozone layer.

Countries in transition will have an environmental agenda which partly overlaps the above. Some of their most urgent problems involve pollution of all kinds, *e.g.*:

- industrial and urban waste disposal;
- water pollution from industrial effluent and untreated sewage;
- air pollution from industry, domestic heating and automobiles;
- cleaning and rehabilitating sites of former military bases;
- acid rain damage to crops, trees and buildings.

However, pollution is not their only concern. Depending on their geographical circumstances and stage of development they may have other environmental concerns, *e.g.*:

- salinisation and waterlogging in irrigated farming;
- the sustainability of intensive farming systems (appropriateness of agro-chemicals, mechanised production, monocropping, waste disposal, etc.);
- preservation of areas of natural beauty and biodiversity;

Developing countries span a wide range of different circumstances. In low-income countries mainly dependent on their natural resource base, a range of other concerns come into play, *e.g.*:

- loss of tropical forest caused by farmers and loggers;
- soil erosion in hill farming, and resulting downstream siltation;
- overgrazing of pastures;
- desertification and dryland degradation;
- abuse of pesticide;
- loss of soil fertility in traditional shifting cultivation;
- drinking water pollution;
- provision of basic sanitation;
- local air pollution from particulates.

Middle income and rapidly industrializing countries in Latin America and Asia will have a range of concerns similar to those of developed or transitional countries, revolving around problems of rapid urban development, industrialisation without proper environmental safeguards, the sustainability of intensive farming systems, the development of new water sources, etc.

In general, the poorer the country, the more likely are local environmental concerns to crowd their agenda and occupy their budgets. Transnational issues such as joint use of international waters, acid rain, and overfishing, will be high on national agenda where vital issues are at stake. Global concerns such as the Greenhouse Effect, Ozone Layer, and biodiversity often seem abstract and remote to countries with pressing local concerns. Countries of all kinds are prepared to commit themselves to these causes where the costs and benefits of programmes in these areas are adequately shared.

Table 3.1. **Environmental Issues and Valuation Methods**

Environmental issues	Productivity	Health	Amenity	Existence
Green (natural resources)				
Soil erosion and fertility	●			
Land degradation	●		●	
Desertification	●			●
Salinisation	●			
Deforestation	●		●	●
Loss of habitats (incl. wetlands)	●		●	●
Wildlife	●		●	●
Depletion of finite resources	●			
Brown (pollution)				
Air pollution	●	●	●	
Waste disposal	●	●	●	
Hazardous waste	●	●	●	
Congestion, noise	●	●	●	
Blue (water-related)				
Groundwater depletion, contamination	●	●	●	
Surface water pollution	●	●		●
Marine environment	●		●	●
Overfishing	●			●
Global				
Global warming, ozone layer	●	●	●	●
Biodiversity, species loss	●		●	●

Each of the above issues can trigger one or more of four categories of impact, on **productivity, health, amenity, or "existence"**. For instance, soil erosion has an obvious potential effect on the productivity of agriculture. Deforestation may affect not only productivity (loss of the value of forest products and services) but also amenity (landscape, local climatic effects) and existence values (forest creatures and species). Air pollution can have an impact on productivity (the cost of defensive measures, impact on trees and crops, corrosion of buildings), health, and amenity (dirt, visibility). The loss of biodiversity affects existence values, but may also reduce amenity (to wildlife lovers) and even productivity (*e.g.* if it reduces tourism or royalties paid by research institutes).

Table 3.1 relates the various kinds of impact to each of a number of key environmental issues. The categories are meant to be illustrative, and not definitive - for instance, soil erosion may also have an impact on amenity through the modification of landscapes, and on health if it results in local food shortages, but its impact on productivity is considered to be its main effect.

So far, this chapter has examined a range of environmental **problems** and has summarized their possible **impacts**. It is now necessary to introduce the possible **valuation methods**, before, finally, reviewing which method is suitable for tackling a particular problem.

3.2. Choice of Valuation Techniques

The three main kinds of valuation method, explained further in Chapters 5, 6, and 7, are:

- using market prices for the physical effects of environmental change on production;
- the use of stated preferences (what people say their environmental values are);
- various kinds of revealed preferences (inferences drawn from peoples' actual behaviour).

i) *Market valuation of physical effects* (MVPE)

This method values environmental change by observing physical changes in the environment and estimating what difference they will make to the value of goods and services. Water pollution may reduce fishing catches, and air pollution can affect the growth of crops. In these cases, environmental changes reduce marketed output. In other cases, such as clearing silt from reservoirs and ditches, environmental change raises costs. In either event, the change costs someone money.

Within the MVPE category, several techniques are available. **Dose-response** measures estimate the physical impact of an environmental change on a receptor, such as air pollution on materials corrosion, acid rain on crop yield, or water pollution on the health of swimmers. **Damage functions** use dose-response data to estimate the economic cost of environmental change. The physical impact caused by environmental change is converted to economic values using the market prices of the units of output.

Under the **production function** approach, environmental "inputs" such as soil fertility and air and water quality can be related through econometric techniques to output, showing how output varies with changes in the various kinds of input. The **human capital** method estimates the cost of bad health resulting from environmental change, according to its effect on the productivity of the worker.

The **replacement cost** method estimates the cost of environmental damage by using the costs which the injured parties incur in putting the harm right, either by observing what the victims actually spend or by consulting expert opinion on what it would cost to remedy the problem.

ii) *Stated preference methods*

In certain situations it is appropriate to ask people directly what their environmental valuations are. **The contingent valuation method** (CVM) is the term given to a form of market research, where the "product" is a change in the environment. People are asked what they would be willing to pay for a hypothetical environmental improvement, or to prevent a deterioration, or what they would be willing to accept in compensation.

CVM may apply equally to changes in public goods, such as air quality, landscape, or the existence values of wildlife, as to goods and services sold to individuals, such as improved water supply and sewerage. It may apply both to **use** values (*e.g.* water quality, viewing wild animals, direct enjoyment of a view) or **non-use** values (existence values).

iii) *Revealed preference methods*

Under this group of techniques, peoples' preferences for the environment are inferred indirectly by examining their behaviour in markets that are linked to the environment. Some goods and services are complements to environmental quality, others are proxies, surrogates or substitutes for it. By examining the prices they pay, or the benefits they apparently derive, in these closely-related markets, peoples' environmental preferences can be uncovered.

There are three principal techniques. The **travel cost method (TCM)** uses the time and cost incurred in visiting and enjoying a natural site as a proxy measure of the price of entering it. **Avertive behaviour (AB)** and **defensive expenditure (DE)** obtain information from what people are observed to spend to protect themselves against an actual or potential decline in their environmental quality.

The **hedonic pricing method (HPM)** starts from the fact that the price of a property reflects, amongst other things, the quality of the environment in which it is located. Applied to property, it uses econometric analysis of large data bases to unbundle environmental attributes from the various other factors making up the price of a dwelling or piece of land. The same basic approach can be used to infer the value of different environmental health risks from systematic differences in wages.

All three methods estimate people's revealed preferences from data on their observed market behaviour.

3.3. Matching Valuation Methods to Specific Impacts

For each of the four broad kinds of impacts identified above, different valuation methods are appropriate. The options are set out in Table 3.2.

For an impact on **productivity**, the most obvious method is MVPE, which places a market value on the physical effect on production (*e.g.* loss of crops from acid rain). However, for those impacts that entail increasing costs, AB, DE and RC could also be suitable (*e.g.* cost of relocation to avoid pollution, double glazing to reduce ambient noise, cost of repairs after floods).

For impacts on **health**, including safety, HC and COI provide minimum estimates, based on the loss of earnings and direct medical outlays. AB (*e.g.* relocation by asthmatics to avoid air pollution) and DE (installation of private water treatment to safeguard against contamination) can give additional pointers. The full health impact may be captured by CV surveys, which measure willingness to pay to avoid or reduce the risk of pain and discomfort, as well as monetary losses. The above applies to morbidity. For mortality risks it is now usual to infer the value of a statistical life by examining insurance outlays, or other kinds of defensive expenditure.

To measure **amenity** effects, TCM and HPM provide data based, respectively, on the cost of travel to a site, and differences in property values due to environmental causes. CV can also be used to probe public preferences.

Table 3.2. **Environmental Impacts and Valuation Methods**

Impact	Valuation methods
Productivity	Market valuation of physical effects (MVPE) Avertive behaviour (AB) Defensive expenditure (DE) Replacement cost (RC)
Health	Human capital (HC) or cost of illness (COI) Contingent valuation (CVM) Avertive behaviour Defensive expenditure
Amenity	Contingent valuation Travel cost (TCM) Hedonic property method (HPM)
Existence values	Contingent valuation

CV is the only practical method of uncovering **existence value** (*e.g.* preservation of rare species, biodiversity for its own sake), since all the other methods are concerned with various kinds of direct user benefits and costs. It is also the only source of evidence on the value of **future** changes in environmental quality.

The final step is to read Table 3.2 in combination with Table 3.1 to understand the valuation methods that are available for applying to a specific environmental issue. For instance, Table 3.1 indicates that deforestation is likely to have impacts under the categories productivity, amenity and existence value. Scanning Table 3.2 enables the reader to conclude that, for deforestation, a range of valuation techniques might be suitable – MVPE, CV, AB, DE, RC, TCM, or HPM.

Obviously, not all these methods should be pursued in each case; the choice should be made according to:

• which type of impacts are more prominent;
• what information is available and feasible;
• resources available to the analyst.

Relative prominence of impacts

To persist with the example of deforestation, suppose the problem is the loss of original tropical forest due to a combination of clearance for agriculture or livestock, and selective logging. Suppose also that, following a review of the situation, the analyst decides that the main environmental impacts are likely to be:

i) the loss of non-timber forest values (medicines, nuts, fibres, etc.);
ii) the loss of long term sustainable timber yield (measured by its stumpage value);
iii) downstream siltation and flood risk from soil eroded from the exposed land;
iv) loss of biodiversity and wildlife, affecting existence values and eco-tourism.

Impacts i) and ii) should be tractable with the MVPE and its variants. Impact iii) could be tackled using DE and RC, while impact iv) could be dealt with partly by CV and partly by MVPE insofar as tourism was affected.

Available information

The second factor in the choice of valuation method is the type and amount of information that is available, and the feasibility/cost of obtaining it. The question of information will be raised at greater length in Chapter 4. For the purpose of the present discussion certain general observations can be made. The MVPE is relatively easy to apply (*e.g.* to timber, and tourism) and — for marketable goods and services — data is relatively easy to obtain. For goods and services where markets are thinner and less developed (*e.g.* subsistence foodstuffs, and non-timber forest products) greater ingenuity has to be shown, and some survey work will be entailed into the range of products in question, the uses they are put to, and their substitutes.

Externalities in general, and downstream effects in particular, are difficult to track, except by using simplified models and strong assumptions. The extent of soil erosion from changes in land use can be roughly predicted by feeding data on the local situation into standard soil-loss equations, but modelling the spread of soil downstream is very difficult and in practice data collection would be eclectic, using historical data on sedimentation, anectodal episodes, and experienced expert opinion on DE and RC.

In situations for which other techniques might be potentially useful, it should be noted that both CV and TCM are survey-based methods requiring careful sampling, training of enumerators, and months of preparation and analysis. HPM is the most data-intensive of all, and rules itself out for all but a few valuation exercises.

Resources available for analysis

The method of valuation chosen in a particular situation also depends on the resources available for conducting the exercise. If the valuation is being done as part of a long term research or consultancy study with adequate time and funding, very different considerations apply as compared with a feasibility study for a specific project, with a tight budget and deadline.

Where resources and time are scarce an eclectic approach will be required, using a mixture of evidence from other projects, international data for comparable situations, local expert opinion, historical records, limited surveys of interested parties, etc. Many governments and lending/donor agencies have strict requirements for the assessment of environmental projects, and, increasingly, economic data are being called for as part of these assessments.

Where the schedule for the project cycle is adequate, surveys (*e.g.* for CV, TCM) can be set in motion in time to yield results for the appraisal. Where this is not possible, the analyst should try to ensure that a baseline survey is undertaken, and that a system of monitoring and reporting is included as part of the project, so that relevant information can be generated as the project evolves, with provision for feedback.

Further References and Sources

There are several accessible introductions to environmental valuation:

BARDE, J.-Ph., *Économie et politique de l'environnement*, Presses Universitaires de France, Paris, 1992.

BOJO, J., MALER, K-G and UNEMO, L, *Environment and development: an economic approach*, Kluwer, Dordrecht, 1990, new edition 1993.

DIXON, J.A., FALLON SCURA, L., CARPENTER, R.A. and SHERMAN, P.B., *Economic analysis of environmental impacts*, Earthscan, London, new edition 1994.

MUNASINGHE, M., *Environmental economics and valuation in development decisionmaking*, World Bank Environment Working Paper, No. 51, 1992.

PEARCE, D., MARKANDYA, A. and BARBIER, E., *Blueprint for a green economy*, Earthscan, London, 1989.

WINPENNY, J.T., *Values for the environment: a guide to economic appraisal*, HMSO, London, 1991.

More advanced expositions are contained in the OECD Technical Volume (1994), and in such works as the following (amongst many others):

BRADEN, J.B. and KOLSTAD, C.D. (ed.), *Measuring the demand for environmental quality*, Elsevier Science Publishers B.V., North Holland, Amsterdam, 1991.

DESAIGUES, B. and POINT, P., *Économie du patrimoine naturel, la valorisation des bénéfices de protection de l'environnement*, Economica, Paris, 1993.

FREEMAN, A.M. III, *The measurement of environmental and resource values: theory and methods*, Resources for the Future, 1993.

HUFSCHMIDT, M.M. *et al.*, *Environment, natural systems and development: an economic valuation guide*, Johns Hopkins, 1983.

PEARCE, D. and MARKANDYA, A., *Environmental policy benefits: monetary valuation*, OECD, Paris, 1989.

PEARCE, D. and TURNER, R.K., *Economics of natural resources and the environment*, Harvester Wheatsheaf, UK, 1990.

The following contains specimen case studies of valuation:

DIXON, J. and HUFSCHMIDT, M. (eds.), *Economic valuation techniques for the environment: a case study workbook*, Johns Hopkins, 1986.

The following also contain original, or reviews of, valuation case material:

BARDE, J.-P. and PEARCE, D.W., *Valuing the environment. Six case studies*, Earthscan, London, 1991.

DIXON, J., JAMES, D. and SHERMAN, P., (eds.), *Dryland management. Economic case studies*, Earthscan, London, 1990.

DIXON, J., FALLON SCURA, L., CARPENTER, R., SHERMAN, P., *Economic Analysis of environmental impacts*, Earthcan, London, 1994.

NAVRUD, S. (ed.), *Pricing the European Environment*, Scandinavian University Press/Oxford University Press, Oslo/Oxford/New York.

Chapter 4

SOURCES OF INFORMATION

The choice of environmental data depends on the uses to which it will be put. If the purpose is to monitor overall trends in a country's environment, an arsenal of data is normally available, some of it in a form useful for international comparisons (OECD, 1994). There have been great strides in the development of Geographical Information Systems, including satellite imagery, and their interpretation through "ground truthing". Air and water quality is regularly monitored in many countries. Wildlife and biodiversity is increasingly being tracked and measured, especially by NGOs.

Despite this progress in amassing environmental information, the data situation in many countries, especially the poorer ones, is unsatisfactory. Important decisions are being taken on the basis of information about the environment which is often deplorable, being based on partial evidence, extrapolations from old data or unrepresentative cases, the transfer of evidence from similar situations elsewhere, assumptions and "guesstimates".

This chapter, and the Field Manual as a whole, is written for the benefit of people who have to take decisions about specific projects, programmes and policies (in short, **interventions)** which have consequences for the environment. Information is needed about likely impacts which are specific to a project, location, region, or type of intervention. It is most unlikely, except by happy coincidence, that environmental data collected routinely by governments or NGOs can be adapted for appraisal purposes without a good deal more work.

4.1. Sources of Information

The following are, in practice, likely to be the main sources of information suitable for environmental project and policy appraisal:

- Regular **national and international reports** on environmental indicators. These provide much useful background information, but are unlikely to contain information on specific impacts (Box 4.1).

Box 4.1.   **Reports on Environmental Data and Indicators**

The following are produced regularly, and most of them annually:

– OECD, *Environmental Data* (for OECD members).
– OECD, *Environmental indicators: OECD core set* (1994).
– UNEP, *Environmental Data Report.*
– World Resources Institute (with UNDP and UNEP) *World Resources.*
– UNECE, *The environment in Europe and North America.*

The following also contain relevant economic and social data, systematically presented:

– World Bank, *World Development Report.*
– UNDP, *Human Development Report.*

Individual countries sometimes produce their own regular environmental surveys (state of the environment reports). For developing countries, the following are good sources:

– *National Environmental Action Plans.*
– *National Conservation Strategies.*

A list of major environmental reports, country-by-country, appears in:

– IIED/WRI/IUCN, *Directory of country environmental studies,* 1993.

- Other **national data bases** of more specific relevance. Interventions concerned with specific habitats or problems need more detailed, and geographically restricted, information on the state of the environment and its determinants. GIS data can throw light on trends in the extent of major vegetational zones. Models of river basins, aquifers and coastal waters can be invaluable in predicting future water supplies, water pollution, and the impact of proposed hydraulic works. Predicting the impact of a proposed project, or control measure, on air quality can be helped by models of "airsheds".

- **Environmental impact assessments (EIAs)** are usually commissioned specifically to report on the impact of a particular project or measure. Many governments and international lending/donor agencies have requirements for the provision of EIAs for investments and policies considered to be environmentally sensitive. The scope and terms of reference for EIAs are normally available from the client agency, and differ accordingly, though they usually cover a common list of subjects (Box 4.2).

EIAs are normally concerned with physical impacts (on the natural environment and animal and human receptors) rather than with their social and economic

Box 4.2. **Environmental Impact Assessments**

EIAs, which are here regarded as the same as environmental assessments, commonly need to cover the following points, amongst others:

- background information, including: description of proposed project; characteristics, and limits, of the study area; history of the proposal; the main interested parties; an account of the alternatives that have been considered, etc.;
- description of the environment of the proposed project: its physical, biological and socio-cultural features; trends and threats to the environment; analysis of the causes of problems identified; assessment of available environmental data, and recommendations on improving it;
- compilation of legislative and regulatory factors relevant to the case, including legislation on environmental quality, health and safety, conservation and protection of habitats and species, physical planning and land use measures, etc. National policy statements and international commitments are also relevant;
- assessment of potential environmental impacts of project: direct and indirect, immediate and long term, significant and minor; local and distant. Rank according to their size and severity, using quantitative measures (and economic values) where possible. Emphasise effects which are irreversible. Draw attention to areas of uncertainty, and assess the extent and quality of available data;
- analyse alternatives. Identify and appraise alternative means of achieving the objectives of the project, including design, location, timing, construction options, O & M procedures, etc., where these alternatives are likely to have significantly different environmental impacts. The option of not proceeding with the project should also be included, to illustrate the "without project" impact. These alternatives should be quantified and appraised, even if roughly;
- consider mitigation measures. For the preferred choice, consider and recommend measures to reduce negative impacts to acceptable levels, including: any changes to laws or regulations; design modifications; relocation; rescheduling; resettlement or compensation to injured parties; imposition of taxes, charges, subsidies to redistribute costs and benefits. The financial and economic costs of these measures should be estimated;
- set out the institutional implications of carrying out the preferred project, with the recommended mitigating measures. These would include any new legislation or regulations, new agencies or reforms to existing ones, new bureaucratic or management functions, new financial authority, personnel and training needs, etc.;
- stipulate monitoring and evaluation needs, including baseline surveys, definition of environmental performance and impact indicators, recommendations for frequency and type of monitoring and feedback, etc.

Source: World Bank Sourcebook, ODA Manual.

implications. They should be regarded as sources of the raw environmental data on which economists and others subsequently work. However, it is highly desirable that terms of reference for EIAs should be cleared by economists and other social scientists so that they will include data necessary for appraisal purposes

- **Environmental audits** on individual firms, government departments or operations. Firms operating in countries with stringent environmental legislation have become highly sensitive to their legal liabilities. The same awareness is extending, though more slowly, to public sector concerns, which can no longer regard themselves as above the law. There is an active market in the provision of audits which indicate the impact of current, or prospective, activities on the environment, and the firm's potential liability. This is particularly important for new products and processes, where a change in the law is imminent, where the law applies retrospectively, where a company is taking over another, etc. Audits are normally confidential to the client, for obvious reasons, but some firms see fit to publish them, and those that are germane to a public investment decision should be accessible, if used with discretion.

- **Appraisal and feasibility reports** by consultants on the project or policy under scrutiny. If time permits, the analyst may be able to commission consultants to assemble the necessary information, including carrying out surveys. A consultancy is as long as a piece of string, but studies of 2-6 months are typical, and the shorter ones can normally be fitted into the schedule (and budget) of a typical project cycle.

- **Research**. In some cases – *e.g.* a large and exceptionally complex project, or an important question of policy – may justify mounting a research programme to examine the issue in depth. The duration of research projects is normally measured in years rather than months, but for some issues a long lead time for study and preparation might be appropriate. Another possible situation is where the generation of data is part of the ongoing aims of the project, *e.g.* a pilot scheme, or one that is phased, with intensive data collection as part of monitoring and feedback. Some major consultancies take several years and the information they assemble could also be regarded as a kind of applied research.

Any of the above data sources are potentially available to the analyst. Some, *e.g.* EIAs and appraisal reports, may be specially commissioned for the task in hand. The remainder of this section offers possible guidance on decisions about where to get data and how much to spend on its collection, and how the various kinds of information can be used in typical situations.

4.2. Data: Where to Get it and How Much to Spend

Since our knowledge of environmental matters is generally poor, it is tempting to spend whatever is necessary to procure enlightenment. Tempting, but infeasible. There is no denying that better information is a benefit that will improve the design of projects and the quality of decision-making, a factor that economists recognise in the concepts of option and quasi-option values. But information has a significant cost of production, and the time it takes is an opportunity cost. It is simply not feasible to get the maximum or the best data for every single piece of appraisal.

The analyst, faced with pressing time and budgetary constraints, and urgent environmental problems, needs to make difficult judgements about where it is best to invest in information, and how much to spend in pursuit of it. In some cases, the client – or the laws of the country – will have certain requirements which effectively dictate the information that is collected. The study may also have a budget (typically, a given percentage of the cost of the project) which affects the amount of data it is feasible to gather. However, even where data requirements are laid down and the study budget is fixed, there is room for choice over data sources and the effort devoted to their pursuit.

Sensitivity and switching analysis (Chapter 2) can be used to identify those elements in the project to which its performance is most closely linked, and to which it is most vulnerable. Where an EIA has been performed, this information can be compared to that resulting from the sensitivity analysis to indicate those types of environmental data likely to have the greatest impact on the project (*e.g.* the success of investment in prawn production is very sensitive to water quality). The EIA may also indicate the major potential legal liabilities of the project sponsor, or the areas in which civil damage suits might be forthcoming. Any further information on these aspects of the project would clearly be of high value.

The analyst should compare the potential value of various kinds of information with the cost of generating these data. Chapters 5, 6, and 7 below offer general guidance on the cost and difficulty of collecting environmental economic data for the various valuation techniques. For instance, it is unlikely to be sensible to use the hedonic property method to value air or water quality, unless:

- a large data base on property values already exists;
- the analyst has, or has access to, the capability of analysing the data by econometric methods;
- other valuation methods are unsuitable, or data is not available;
- the effect in question (*e.g.* air quality) is critical to the decision being taken.

Once it is decided to collect more information on certain environmental values, the next decision is whether to gather original data specific to that project, or whether to cast around in an eclectic fashion for data produced elsewhere that can be adapted for the current purpose. In short, should data be project-specific or drawn from elsewhere?

Some of the considerations involved in the collection of project-specific data have already been aired. Before a decision is made, the feasibility of using relevant data generated elsewhere should be explored. A specific aspect of this is the growing practice of benefit transfer.

4.3. Benefit Transfer (BT)

BTs apply a data set developed for one particular use to a quite distinct alternative situation. In a very general sense, where data on environmental values in a specific project and/or locality are absent, it is common to borrow unit values developed elsewhere to illustrate orders of magnitude. The non-timber values of tropical rain forest, estimated from detailed surveys in a few parts of the Amazon, West Africa and South-East Asia, have been widely quoted to illustrate the potential values of other tracts of forest. A number of studies use empirical relationships on afforestation and soil fertility, or soil erosion and crop yield, developed in specific areas, more widely to "slot into" exercises where local empirical data is not available.

However, BT has come to mean something more specific. It usually applies to non-market values (*e.g.* of air and water quality, or recreation), since these are not so easy to obtain as market values. The location where the data was generated is known as the **study site**, and the project or area that the benefits are transferred to is the **policy site**. In some cases the methodology developed at the study site can be transferred to the policy site, using empirical data at the latter. In other cases, the methodology, data and values are transferred wholesale.

BT is appropriate when certain conditions are present:

- there are insufficient funds, time, or personnel to undertake a satisfactory new study;
- the study site is similar to the policy site;
- the issues (*e.g.* proposed policy change, or nature of project) are similar in the two cases;
- the original valuation procedures were sound and the exercise was done conscientiously.

Box 7.1 (Chapter 7) quotes typical values derived from the large number of travel cost studies of recreational values in the USA, which are often used in BT. Outside the USA and Western Europe there is much less scope for using BT since original studies are very much fewer, and cross-country BTs are problematic. Contingent valuation studies, for instance, are dominated by US literature, with Western

Europe a poor second, and is concentrated on air quality, recreational fishing, forestry, health risks, recreational hunting, parks, nature reserves and wildlife, water quality and water supply. Travel cost studies are mainly to be found in recreational fishing, parks, nature reserves and wildlife, and water supply and quality. Hedonic property studies have been done mainly for air quality, noise and parks, nature reserves and wildlife (OECD, 1994).

Further References and Sources

A full description of environmental data required for project identification and appraisal, sector by sector, is contained in the World Bank's *Environmental Assessment Sourcebook*, in three volumes, which first appeared as World Bank Technical Paper No. 139, 1991. The Sourcebook also contains a sample terms of reference for an Environmental Assessment (Annex 1-3 to Vol. 1).

Most of the other leading development agencies, and some governments, have now produced environmental appraisal guidelines or manuals. The following are quoted as examples of a range that are now available (the reader conducting an appraisal on behalf of a particular agency would be well advised to obtain the agency's own guidelines or requirements):

Overseas Development Administration (UK): *Manual of Environmental Appraisal*, London, 1992 (which also contains suggestions for the content of an Environmental Impact Appraisal).

European Bank for Reconstruction and Development: *Environmental procedures*, London, 1992

Readers seeking more information on benefit transfers should consult the collection of papers on this subject contained in *Water Resources Research*, Vol. 28, No. 3, March 1992.

A detailed chapter is devoted to benefit transfer in OECD *"Project and Policy Appraisal, Integrating Economics and the Environment"*, OECD, Paris, 1994.

See also, Asian Development Bank, *Economic Assessment of Environmental Impacts, a workbook*, (forthcoming).

Chapter 5

THE MARKET VALUATION OF PHYSICAL EFFECTS

5.1. The Concept

The most straightforward way of valuing environmental change is to observe physical changes in the environment and estimate what difference they will make to the value of goods and services. Acid rain causes damage to trees and plants, which reduces their market value. Soil erosion reduces the yield of crops grown on site, and may cause downstream farmers and reservoir owners to spend more on removing silt from their property. In these cases, environmental changes cost someone money.

The three basic steps entailed in the market valuation of physical effects (MVPE) method are:

- Firstly, estimate the physical effect of the environmental change on the **receptor** (the property, machine or person affected by the change), *e.g.* upland deforestation may cause soil losses of 3 per cent p.a.

- Secondly, estimate what difference this will make to **output** or costs. A 3 per cent p.a. loss of soil may reduce the output of maize by 2 per cent p.a., say, 100 kg on a typical plot.

- Thirdly, estimate the market value of this change in output or costs. The loss of 100 kg of maize p.a. would cause a net loss of income to the farmer of, say, $250 (100 kg x $3/kg = $300, minus a $50 saving on harvesting and other variable costs).

Various methods are used in MVPE:

- **Dose-response** measures estimate the physical impact of an environmental change on a receptor, such as air pollution on materials corrosion, acid rain on crop yield, or water pollution on the health of swimmers.

- **Damage functions** use dose-response data to estimate the economic cost of environmental change. The physical impact caused by environmental change is converted to economic values using the market prices of the units of output.

- The **production function** approach. A common economic technique is to relate output to different levels of inputs of the so-called factors of production (land, labour, capital, raw materials). A change in the use of one of these (say, labour) will produce a certain change in output. Production is said to be a **function** of these inputs, and is related to them algebraically. Environmental "inputs" such as soil fertility and air and water quality can be included as inputs where they can be measured, and where they have a clear effect on output (*e.g.* the saline content of irrigation water is one of the influences on crop yield, along with the quantity of water, amount of seed, fertilizer, labour, etc.).

- The **human capital** method estimates the cost of bad health resulting from environmental change. Evidence is sought from epidemiological data, control group experiments, or other observations about the likely effect of environmental quality on human health. The economic cost of bad health is obtained by estimating its effect on the productivity of the worker. The term "human capital" is applied because only the value of a person as a working unit is considered in this calculation (the person's subjective valuation of health, his/her willingness to pay for better health, the cost of pain and suffering, etc. are not reckoned in this context, though they are obviously important).

- **Replacement cost** is a special case of the same approach. In this case, the damage cost of environmental change is estimated by the costs which the injured parties incur in putting the harm right. The data can be obtained either by observing what the victims actually spend (*e.g.* building walls and bunds to protect farms against the deposition of silt) or by consulting expert opinion on what it would cost to remedy the problem.

The term "damage function" does not imply that this technique is solely concerned with valuing **costs**. Some environmental changes have positive effects on marketed output, *e.g.* creating a new reservoir also creates a fishery, reducing the discharge of sewage off a popular beach increases income from tourism and fishing, etc. In such cases the environment-output link may not be robust enough to use a dose-response relationship. Nevertheless, it would be reasonable to expect environmental change to benefit output, and the MVPE approach is valid.

MVPE is sometimes called a "short cut" method because it proceeds straight to estimating the impact of environmental change on the receptor concerned. Unlike the techniques discussed in Chapters 6 and 7, it is not concerned with what people say they prefer, or inferring environmental values indirectly from what they are observed to do.

5.2. When is this Technique Appropriate?

The approach has widespread application. In practice, it is by far the most common valuation method in countries at all stages of development. It appeals to intuition and common sense, and is easy to explain and justify.

It can be applied to the following kinds of problems and issues:

- the effect of soil erosion on crop yield and the impact of resulting downstream siltation on other users of the watershed (*e.g.* lowland farmers, irrigators, water utilities, power companies, river and estuary navigators);

- the effects of acid rain on the growth, stunting and blemishing of crops and trees, and its effect on the corrosion and tarnishing of materials and equipment;

- damage from air pollution to human health, due to the presence of air-borne particulates or other harmful substances;

- the impact of water pollution on human health, *e.g.* the effect of faecal coliforms on skin and intestinal disorders, or of water-borne diseases spread by reservoirs and irrigation systems;

- salinisation of irrigated land due to poor drainage and water-logging, affecting crop yields;

- the climatic and ecological effects of afforestation;

- the change of land from one use to another, *e.g.* the conversion of a natural habitat into farmland or livestock pasture, leading to the loss of natural products offsetting the benefits from the new land use;

- the accumulation of heavy metal and other dangerous chemical residues in the soil and groundwater bodies, due to discharges from mines, farms and waste disposal sites.

Valuing physical effects is appropriate in the following circumstances:

- the environmental change directly causes an increase or decrease in the output of a good (or service) which is marketed, or is potentially marketable, or which has a close substitute which is marketed;

- the effect is clear and can be observed, or tested empirically;

- markets function well, so that the price is a good indicator of economic value.

5.3. Determining the Physical Impact

Data can be obtained from a number of different sources:

a) laboratory or field research (e.g. effect of marine pollution on fisheries through its effect on reef ecology; effect of overfishing on fish populations); observing the effect of air pollution on crops or materials corrosion);

b) controlled experiments, in which the effect is deliberately induced (e.g. agronomic trials on land with different degrees of erosion, or with different applications of pesticide; exposing animals to chemical contamination or air pollution); making observations on receptors with and without the effect by using control groups as the norm;

c) statistical regression techniques that try to isolate the influence of a particular effect from that of a number of others. This is common in health research, where there would be objections to direct experiments with people;

d) relationships can be modelled, based on plausible information drawn from real life. In soil erosion studies, for instance, it is common to use some variant of the Soil Loss Equation, which predicts erosion according to slope, rainfall, soil type and a dummy variable for management practices and type of crop. A further link then needs to be established between erosion and yield.

5.4. Attaching Market Values

The easiest approach is to use ruling market prices to value changes in production. This is reasonable if the change in output is not so large that it is likely to affect prices, and if the price is at a market-clearing level.

Complications arise when the change in output is on such a scale that prices are likely to be affected. A large part of national supply might come from the area affected by pollution or erosion. Local markets may be badly linked with those in the rest of the country (*e.g.* local markets for fresh fish). In such cases, some attempt should be made to predict changes in prices.

The use of actual prices would also be misleading if markets were seriously distorted by monopoly, price controls, or protection against imports. For instance, if the crop that is subject to soil erosion is kept at an artificially high support price, using prevailing prices would overestimate the real environmental damage. If possible, prices should be adjusted to their market-clearing, or competitive, levels.

The method can also apply to output which is not actually marketed, but where an actual market exists for similar goods, or substitutes. In studies of tropical deforestation, a problem is that many forest products are used for subsistence purposes and are not sold on markets. One approach is to take the price of a close substitute, or a commercial variety of the traditional item (*e.g.* a commercial medicine as a proxy for a traditional cure). However, none of the ways of getting round the problem of absent markets is fully satisfactory.

For the sake of accuracy and realism, the **net** effect of output and price changes should be estimated. Multiplying the change in units of output by their price yields a gross sum which should be adjusted for any resulting changes in costs to produce the net result on incomes or value-added. For instance, if soil erosion reduces the output of a crop, there will be partially offsetting savings in harvesting costs. The opposite situation is where environmental damage causes an increase in the cost of an item, as well as reducing its output (*e.g.* if it takes longer to catch fewer fish in polluted water).

5.5. Applications

The remainder of this chapter describes and assesses the use of this method in six situations, each representing a globally important problem. These are:

- measuring the cost of soil erosion;
- tracing the link between air pollution and bad health;
- assessing the health effects of irrigated rice farming;
- adding the benefits of reducing sedimentation;
- justifying afforestation schemes;
- quantifying the cost of depleting soil nutrients.

i)   Measuring the cost of soil erosion

Studies of the economic cost of soil erosion are demonstrating that many conventional farming systems are in reality depleting the fertility of their land, and this "depreciation" is in many cases wiping out apparent production gains. Studies in various African countries estimate that the underlying decline in soil fertility caused by erosion could well lie in the range 5-10 of national farm income. In Java, Indonesia, the annual costs of soil erosion were estimated to be about 4 per cent of the value of annual crop production (Repetto *et al.*, 1989).

The problem is not confined to developing countries. In the USA studies of the combined on-site and off-site costs of soil erosion in two states show that "alternative" farming systems can be competitive with, or even superior to, conventional practices when full account is taken of the private and national costs of erosion and sedimentation (Faeth *et al.*, 1991).

The first step in applying MVPE to this problem is to estimate the extent of soil erosion. Because this is difficult to measure, and is determined by a number of factors, soil scientists have developed a general estimator which has proved helpful in indicating orders of magnitude for erosion in certain conditions. This is the Universal Soil Loss Equation, applicable to agricultural land with slopes of less than 50 degrees.

In its basic form, the USLE relates soil loss to four main factors – rainfall erosiveness, soil erodibility, topography and vegetation management (erosion control). A modified USLE has been developed to cater for non-agricultural land with a variety of vegetation on steeper slopes. The collection of the necessary data for the USLE from local farmers is a manageable undertaking, and the Equation provides useful results for a range of typical conditions.

Different types of vegetation can produce startling differences in soil loss rates. Measurements carried out on slopes in Thailand demonstrate average annual loss of up to 10 tonnes per square kilometre under natural forest or flat paddy, over 1 000 tonnes for mixed forest, rubber plantations, orchards and paddy, and over 100 000 tonnes for mixed field crops, forest, and unstable shifting cultivation. It should be stressed that these results would not necessarily apply to a radically different situation, *e.g.* more gentle slopes and moderate rainfall.

Once some estimate of the **amount** of soil erosion is available, the next step is to estimate its effect on the productivity of farming systems. Some level of "soil loss" (its so-called T-value) has little significant effect on productivity, depending on the initial status of the soil, organic matter content, parent material, climate, available soil, water, etc.

However, if annual losses persist they will eventually affect soil productivity, and any level of erosion is of concern to downstream areas affected by sedimentation.

The relationship between loss of soil and crop yield has been extensively plotted in the United States and to a lesser extent in other temperate countries. For maize, the decline in yield (kg per ha, for each cm of soil loss) ranges from 30 to 268; for wheat from 21 to 54. The relationship depends heavily on the type of soil, its initial depth, slope, crop, and on temperate or tropical location. Erosion appears to have a greater effect on absolute yields in tropical conditions, starting from a lower average base. Soil loss can be very rapid in marginal areas, and after a while soil depth diminishes to a point at which crop growth is not viable, and the land goes out of production.

The final step is to translate yield losses into economic values. The crudest approach is to applying prevailing prices per unit to the physical change in output. However, if prices are expected to change, this should be taken into account. The total impact on farm budgets should be estimated, where data are available. For instance, reduced output of cereals due to erosion may save some harvesting costs, but may have repercussions on livestock through reduced forage supply, and on household fuel and fertiliser bills through a reduced supply of residues. A further complication arises where farms anticipate erosion, and take precautionary actions, *e.g.* spend more on fertilizer, use dung on the fields rather than as fuel, etc.

This discussion indicates that the MVPE is not as straightforward as it may seem. Nevertheless, its basic elements are clear, and it produces vivid results (Box 5.1.).

ii) *Air pollution and human health*

It is now common knowledge that air pollution can damage the health of people predisposed to certain complaints. However, specifying the damage, quantifying it, and estimating its economic costs are all steps with potential pitfalls, requiring careful handling. This problem is a classic application of dose-response and damage functions.

There are several steps in tracing the link between pollution and health:

- Determine the type and volume of **emission.** Problems could arise in collecting data in rapidly growing cities with many individual polluters from households, small industries, automobiles, etc.

- Estimate pollution **concentrations** at relevant points in the atmosphere. This normally relies on a "dispersion model" to predict the spread of pollutants

Box 5.1.   **Mali: The On-site Cost of Soil Erosion (Bishop and Allen, 1989)**

This study attempted to put a value on the top soil used up in agricultural production. The authors used the USLE to predict erosion and to estimate its effects on crop yields, before working through farm budgets into money values.

Mali is an African state located in the arid and semi-arid Sahelian zone. Most of the population depend on various forms of agriculture and livestock, and the signs of ecological deterioration (reduced rainfall and river levels, loss of forest and pasture, reduced soil fertility and loss of plant and animal species) are potentially very serious.

Soil loss, in tons per ha, was assumed to be a reliable predictor of changes in soil nutrient content, soil pH and moisture retention, which account for almost all the annual variation in yields of maize and cowpeas. Data on the physical characteristics of land was obtained from a detailed atlas based on satellite images, containing data on soil, vegetation, rainfall, groundwater and land use on which detailed land categories were established to provide the essential information to the soil loss equations.

The USLE was used to predict erosion. Most climatic and soil data collected recently in West Africa were intended for use in the USLE and data available in Mali were easily adapted for this. Because of the positive benefits of deposition, soil loss on catchments known to receive significant alluvial deposits was discounted. The relation between erosion and crop yield was estimated using experimental data from Nigeria. Crop yields were, in turn, translated into farm incomes using farm budgets published by ICRISAT for comparable conditions in Burkina Faso. Farm income forgone from erosion was projected forward ten years and discounted at 10 per cent. Results were grossed up for the whole of Mali.

The loss of soil on cultivated land was estimated to be an average of 6.5 t/ha/year for the whole study area, the highest loss being 30 t/ha/year in the Southern zone where rainfall is high and the soil more erodible. The mean present value of farm income forgone over ten years as a result of one year of soil loss ranged from CFAF 2 000-8 000 per ha (average net annual farm revenues, excluding rice, were about CFAF 9 700 per ha). The sacrifice of future revenues from erosion was 2-9 per cent of current farm income. $31 M (4 per cent of farm GDP).

These losses were compared with the costs of various kinds of simple water harvesting measures, such as the construction of bunds and ridges which conserve the soil and help conserve rainfall. The discounted total cost of these techniques was in the range CFAF 40 000-100 000. In many cases the present value of farm income forgone through erosion was greater than the cost of the cheapest conservation technique.

Nationally, annual discounted losses were estimated to be at least US$31 M (4 per cent of agricultural GDP).

This very systematic study used a technique (the USLE) for which local data can be used, and for which erosion-yield relationships and farm budget data were obtained in neighbouring countries. No account was taken of off-site or wider environmental effects (though some adjustment was made for the positive effects of deposition on certain fields). The scale of soil erosion losses is becoming significant to the national economy, and justifies some conservation investment in the worst-affected areas.

from their origin. Pollution sources may be categorised as point or non-point, mobile or stationary, area or line, etc.

- Establish the relationship between specific concentrations of pollutant and human health (**dose-response** studies). Data for the dose-response relationships can be obtained from three main sources. In toxicological studies animal subjects are exposed to high levels of pollutants for short periods in experimental conditions. The results are used to predict human responses. Alternatively, micro epidemiological studies trace the responses of humans to exposure to pollutants over time, compared with control groups not so exposed. Finally, macro epidemiological studies draw upon large data bases to correlate mortality and morbidity with a range of variables, from which pollution can be isolated.

These types of primary data are used to produce a dose-response function which determines how the response or damage (health) is affected by the size of the dose (air pollution). A **linear** function describes a relationship where the damage increases in a constant proportion to the dose. In a **non-linear** function, the relationship changes at different levels of the variables, for instance damage may sharply increase at higher levels of exposure to the dose. The function may display a **threshold**, for instance there may be no effect on health until pollution reaches a critical level. There may also be **discontinuities**, where damage suddenly jumps at a certain critical point of the dose, and then resumes at a linear or non-linear rate.

- Define the **population at risk,** by estimating population within the pollution dispersal "plume", which could extend over large distances. The totals could then be adjusted for sectors of the population especially at risk, for instance, children under 5, asthmatics, people over 70.

There are various ways of quantifying changes in health, *e.g.*:

- deaths;
- number of cases notified;
- number of visits to a doctor;
- number of hospital admissions;
- emergency room visits (ERVs);
- number of asthma attacks;
- number of Restricted Activity Days (RADs);
- number of working days lost, etc.

For the purpose of economic valuation using the MVPE method, the crucial information is of two kinds, namely the cost of ill-health in terms of lost output, and

Box 5.2. **Air Pollution and Health in Jakarta (Dixon *et al*. 1994, Ostro, 1994)**

Jakarta, the capital city of Indonesia, has a population of 8-9 million and suffers serious air pollution. The component of air pollution that is studied in this case is particulate matter (PM). Two types are distinguished – total suspended particulates (TSP) and the more harmful finer particles PM10 (so called because it is particulate matter less than 10 microns in size). Pollution exposure is measured in micrograms of PM per cubic metre (m³) of air. A TSP level of 100 converts to a PM10 of 55.

No dose-response functions are available for Indonesia, hence the researchers use those estimated for developed countries, and assumed that the same relationships could be carried over. The coefficients were applied to local estimates of PM concentrations, and local data on mortality, admissions to respiratory hospitals, emergency room visits, RADs, respiratory illness of children, asthma attacks and chronic disease.

The central purpose of this study was to estimate the economic benefits of reducing TSP levels in Jakarta, currently ranging from 100 to 350 mg/m³ in various parts of the city, to the national standard level (90 mg/m³) and the WHO standard (75 mg/m³). Using coefficients derived from USA and Canada, it as estimated that reducing PM to the national Indonesian standard level would avoid 1 200 premature deaths, and would save 2 000 hospital admissions, 40 000 emergency room visits, and 6 million RADs.

The original study did not place economic values on these results. However, the information is presented in a form that can readily be converted into economic values, on certain assumptions. Both loss of working days and RADs are costed with reference to average wages, which are readily available. The cost of medical care for different types of illness should also be available locally.

More contentiously, standard estimates of the cost of illness developed in the USA could be adopted, suitably scaled down, as a last resort. For instance, in the USA each respiratory hospital admission (RHA) is valued on average at $28 000, made up of a cost of medical care of $26 900 plus a wage rate for each of the 10 days lost of $125. If these data were used, considerable allowance would have to be made for the high medical costs in the USA and the much lower wage rates in Indonesia.

The same goes for the use of US "value of life" estimates. It is now quite common to use peoples' willingness to insure themselves against the risk of illness or death as a proxy for the value of life. Thus, if people would be willing to pay $300 to reduce their risk of death by a factor of 1 in 10 000, it can be inferred that they would value a death avoided at $3 million. Although widely used, this is nevertheless a controversial technique, and the transfer of empirical values from countries as different as the USA and Indonesia is problematic.

costs of medical treatment, both those borne by the victim, and those incurred by the state. The economist needs to have precise pollution-health coefficients, with the health effects suitably quantified, *e.g.* "a 5 per cent increase in the atmospheric concentration of sulphur dioxide will be associated with an x per cent increase in days lost from work due to asthma". The cost of a lost working day or a RAD is normally estimated from average wages, and medical costs per hospital admission can also be obtained.

This so-called **cost-of-illness** approach excludes the cost of pain and suffering and takes no account of what people would be willing to pay to avoid or reduce the risk of illness. Nor is it suitable for dealing with mortality. Even so, it can provide illustrations of the economic costs of pollution-related illness which are useful for policymakers (Box 5.2)

iii) Irrigation and health

Hundreds of millions of people suffer from one or more of the major water-related diseases, such as malaria, schistosomiasis (bilharzia), roundworm, trachoma, guinea worm and other intestinal disorders. Most attention has focused on the effects of major hydraulic works, such as the creation of reservoirs and large irrigation schemes, which create habitats in which vectors can thrive, and in which humans can acquire and transmit diseases. However, any modification in the way water is used can have potential effects on health. For instance, there has been a resurgence of malaria in some African cities, related to the increase In household back-yard irrigation.

The link between environmental change, in this case modifications to the water habitat, and health can be handled in a dose-response framework similar to that used in the above air pollution example. The basic procedure is similar, namely:

- establish the facts about what is happening to the environment (*e.g.* creation of large new fresh water bodies);

- gather data on possible effects on health, drawn from comparable situations elsewhere, or – in the case of an ongoing scheme – historical data from the area in question;

- estimate the economic costs of the predicted incidence of illness, using both working time lost and the direct cost of treatment.

Even this approach, which is the most straightforward, is difficult and demands good data which is rare in tropical conditions. As proof of this, there are very few economic studies of the effects of irrigation on human health. We must also enter caveats about the use of the "cost of illness" approach. Although it is often the only feasible method, it ignores pain and suffering, and disregards what sufferers might be willing to pay to avoid it. Box 5.3 contains a relevant case study.

Box 5.3.   **Irrigation, Health and Farm Output in Cameroon (Audibert, 1986)**

This is a study of the Department of Mayo Danai in the north of Cameroon which was the subject of a World Bank-funded irrigation project begun in the early 1970s and extended in 1979. By 1986 12 600 families worked on the scheme, which covered some 6 800 ha. Rice was the predominant irrigated crop, on a typical plot of 0.5 ha. Many farmers also kept on their old farms, based on millet, fishing and livestock.

The irrigation is managed by a public corporation which provides the main farm services, buys the output, and deducts the cost of services from the price – which is fixed by the government. Records have been kept of the output of each grower and the health status of farmers has been examined and recorded. Seasonally-transmitted malaria is endemic to the region. The prevalence of urinary bilharziasis varies from 10 to 60 per cent according to the village.

All relevant determinants of the level of rice production were taken into account. (In econometric terms, a generalised production function was estimated, and the marginal effect of health status was measured by the coefficient of its variation in the estimated function). The study related the output of rice on each farm plot to a number of possible explanatory variables. It took into account:

- experience of the farmer, measured by the number of previous growing seasons that the family had taken part in;
- size of the labour force available to the family;
- prevalence of malaria and/or bilharziasis;
- duration of transplanting;
- cultivated area;
- rice variety (in statistical terms, a dummy variable);
- number of millet fields cultivated (since millet and rice compete for the family's attention at certain times).

The level of farm inputs was assumed to be the same for all plots, which were mostly of the same size. Likewise the amount of irrigation water and the way it was managed was excluded from analysis on the grounds that these were matters handled by the public irrigation agency. The skill of the individual farmers was difficult to capture in a quantitative exercise of this kind, and in any case its impact on farm-to-farm variations in output was muted by the control and advice exercised by the irrigation agency through its agricultural monitors and irrigation technicians.

No significant difference was noted in the prevalence of malaria between rice-growers on irrigated plots and other people. Nor was the prevalence of malaria a significant explanatory variable for rice output. This was probably because malaria was endemic throughout the region, and it was the type which caused bouts of illness which made people unable to work for short periods. However, schistosomiasis was much more prevalent among people working in flooded paddy fields. This caused debilitation, which specifically affected farmers' ability to transplant. The correlation showed that a 10 per cent increase in the prevalence of schistosomiasis resulted in a 4.9 per cent fall in output.

(continued on next page)

(continued)

The study provided evidence for the argument that poor health affects the output of rice through two principal factors. It influences the area that a family can cultivate – since rice growing is arduous and labour-intensive. It also affects the duration of transplanting of seedlings, which is a crucial stage, best kept short.

This study claims to be the first attempt to relate health to the productivity of self-employed farmers; a few previous studies attempted the same for plantation workers, though with less clear-cut results. The research was carried out 12-15 years after the project started, when trends in health had clearly emerged.

This case study illustrates several key points:

- the importance of taking due account of all the possible influences on output, and "controlling" for them, in order to isolate the effect of health;

- data on health status and output for each farmer were available for a long period. This was highly fortuitous for this kind of study;

- the study has an important feed-back into the future design of this, and other irrigation schemes. It proves that neglect of health impacts can harm both the social **and** the economic performance of the project. It also indicates the value of including the collection and monitoring of all relevant data in the design of major projects of this kind.

iv) *The economics of sedimentation*

Sedimentation is one of the main side-effects of soil erosion. most of the costs of erosion, considered in the first part of this chapter, are those confronted by the farmers themselves, on their own land. Sedimentation is a classic externality, arising from the transport and deposition of soil in other areas. It may confer benefits, in the form of fertile alluvial silt in valley-bottom lands. In other cases siltation causes inconvenience and costs, namely:

- increased risk of flooding;
- interference with navigation in rivers and estuaries;
- siltation of reservoirs, causing losses of irrigation and drinking water, and reduction of hydroelectric potential;

- deposition of coarse material on fields lower down the catchment;
- blockage of irrigation channels;
- loss of drinking water sources through siltation, and use of scarce water for flushing purposes.

The main problem in costing sedimentation is generating the physical information on the transport and deposition of soil particles in the different parts of a catchment. Clearly, the further sediment is transported from its point of erosion, the more difficult it is to predict the location and volume of deposition. The process can take many years, there are many possible sediment traps, much erosion is from natural weathering processes rather than human agency, etc.

The example in Box 5.4 shows how the economic costs of sedimentation can be estimated in a region where tens of millions of people are exposed to the problem.

Comments on case study

- The analysis applies market valuation to the estimated physical environmental effects of a project, namely the reduction in sedimentation from carrying out upstream and on-farm works and farming practices. Benefits are treated as avoided costs, namely the savings from reduced sedimentation.

- One of the benefits, reduced irrigation maintenance, is similar to the concept of *preventive or defensive expenditure*, which is discussed in Chapter 7. It is sometimes difficult to uphold the distinction between preventing a further deterioration in the environment (as in this case) and defending oneself from the consequences of environmental change (which is true preventive expenditure).

- Although the benefits turned out to be large in absolute terms, their inclusion only raised the project's Internal Rate of Return from 19 per cent to 22 per cent. This implies that reckoning the downstream externalities of the project would make relatively little difference to its justification, which turns on its on-site benefits.

- The value of the analysis is twofold. It provides information which could form the basis of cost-sharing for the project between upstream and downstream provinces and the central government. It also indicates the relative cost-effectiveness of different methods of controlling sedimentation.

Box 5.4. **Sedimentation in the Yellow River Basin of China**
(Magrath, 1992, Dixon *et al.*, 1994)

Due to erosion in the Yellow River Basin, a huge amount of sediment (1.6 billion tons) is delivered annually to the lower reaches of the river, much of which (1.1 billion tons) enters the Yellow Sea. 300-400 million tons of sediment are deposited in the lower reaches, and 100-200 million tons are left in the irrigation systems of this region.

Three particular effects of sedimentation are of concern to the Chinese:

- Increased danger of flooding. The river bed rises from 8-10 cm annually, and major dikes have been built to contain the river, which on average is 3-5 metres above its surrounding plain. Every 10-15 years major outlays are incurred to raise the level of the dykes. Any breach would cause unimaginable losses of life and property to this highly productive farming region.
- Damage to irrigation systems. Around half of the 150 million tons of sediment that fills irrigation systems is removed by dredging and other means.
- Costs of water used for flushing sediment out of the lower parts of the river basin and adjacent systems. This water has a high value in other uses.

This study examined various methods of controlling sedimentation through upstream and on-farm works in the Loess Plateau region. These included the trapping of sediment through gulley plugs, check dams and warp dams, land terracing, and the spread of afforestation and grassland. Apart from the on-farm and local benefits of these schemes (*e.g.* on soil fertility, direct products, etc.) the benefits of the work on downstream sedimentation were estimated. In effect, the benefits of the upstream and on-farm project were regarded as the avoided costs of the three problems mentioned above.

It was estimated that the project would reduce the annual flow of sediment into the Yellow River by 41 million tons, or by *c.* 2.6 per cent. The various types of intervention (terracing, forestry, conservation tillage, etc.) were each ascribed a proportion of the sediment savings. The final step was to estimate the avoided costs of sedimentation for each of the three problems noted above.

The first benefit is the postponement of the need to raise dykes. The reservoir of the Xiaolongdi Dam would trap a cumulative total of 7.55 billion tons of sediment; on past performance 22 per cent of this would have reached the river bed, hence the benefit would arise on only 22 per cent of the sediment trapped. The avoided cost of raising dykes along the river were estimated to be RMB Yuan 0.17 per ton of sediment.

The avoided cost of reduced irrigation system maintenance was calculated starting with the fact that in the late 1980s the annual cost of removing 67 million tons of sediment was *c.* RMB Yuan 100 million. This average cost per ton was applied to the proportion of sediment that normally found its way into the irrigation systems, yielding a value of RMB Yuan 0.15 per ton.

(continued on next page)

(continued)

Finally, there is the value of water which would no longer be required for flushing the sediment out of the river and irrigation systems. This is the most difficult benefit to estimate, since the value of the water would vary from place to place, and between one time and another. In short, its opportunity cost would vary unpredictably, according to whether the saved water could be diverted for agricultural or industrial use. Depending on these local circumstances, the value of water saved could vary from zero to RMB Yuan 14.74 per ton of sediment.

Because of the great variability of the water benefits, it is impossible to give a firm estimate of the avoided costs of reduced sedimentation. The avoided costs of dyke raising and irrigation maintenance give a combined benefit of RMB Yuan 0.24/ton. For the purpose of analysis, this was raised to RMB Yuan 1.0/ton.

v)   The case for afforestation

Until recently, it was difficult to provide an economic justification for planting trees. Trees grow so slowly that their benefits arise long into the future. Applying conventional discount rates to their stream of benefits tends to yield an unacceptable economic rate of return. As a result, afforestation schemes are usually undertaken in response to tax incentives, or are subject to a specially low discount rate. There are exceptions, such as rapidly-growing species and trees planted for social and amenity purposes.

However, the growing awareness of the non-timber benefits of trees, especially in developing countries, has led to attempts to place economic values on this wider range of benefits. Estimating the value of the direct products of trees, such as fruit, fodder, mulch/fertiliser and firewood is relatively straightforward. These products either have a market value in their own right (firewood, fruit) or substitute for something else that is marketed (e.g. vegetation used for compost or fertiliser).

More problematic is the estimation of the indirect benefits of trees, such as shade, windbreaks, soil retention, etc. A growing amount of empirical research and trials, especially on agro-forestry, has generated data which is available for economic valuation purposes. The case study in Box 5.5 illustrates how this can be done.

Comments on case study

This was one of the first studies to demonstrate that afforestation **can** be justified according to conventional cost-benefit criteria, despite the lags involved in the

Box 5.5. **Nigeria: Shelterbelts and Farm Forestry (Anderson, 1987)**

The study is a cost-benefit analysis of the tree-planting programme already under way in the arid zone of Northern Nigeria. This region has a typical annual rainfall ranging from 200 to 800 mm and a long dry season. Fuelwood is used for cooking by 90 per cent of the population, at a rate well above the Mean Annual Increment of timber stocks. This is leading to a sharp decline in farm tree stocks, increased encroachment by farmers on public reserves, and the non-sustainable harvesting of trees in the more humid southern belt.

All this threatens to reduce soil fertility through gulley erosion, loss of topsoil, surface evaporation, reduced soil moisture and the use of dung and residues for fuel rather than fertiliser. Storm damage to crops is also becoming more severe.

The afforestation project has support from the World Bank and other agencies. Its two main components are shelterbelts and farm forestry. **Shelterbelts** consist of lines of trees (usually eucalyptus and neem) arranged in 6 to 8 rows up to 10 km long. **Farm forestry** is that undertaken by farmers on their own land, and typically 15-20 trees per ha are planted with the aim of providing useful products (fodder, fruit, fuel, as well as shelter) for the farm households.

The benefits of the programme are perceived as:

- halting future declines in soil fertility;
- improving current levels of soil fertility;
- the value of the tree products themselves;
- increasing the supply of fodder.

Following a review of a large body of international research, it is assumed that shelterbelts would increase the net yield of crops in the vicinity by 15-25 per cent. The main mechanisms for this would be increasing soil moisture retention, reducing crop losses from wind, and reducing surface wind speeds. For farm forestry the increased yield is taken to be a more modest 5-10 per cent.

The impact of shelterbelts is assumed to occur 7 to 10 years after planting, and for farm forestry 8 to 13 years. These "with project" benefits are compared with the assumed trend "without", which is a decline in soil fertility of 0-2 per cent p.a. This decline would be halted after 8 years with the project. The value of wood and fruit from the new trees is estimated to be $22 per ha for the shelterbelts and $7 for the farm forestry, both net of labour costs. The major investment costs of the programme are:

- fencing and planting expenses, amounting to *c.* $150 per ha of protected land for shelterbelts and $40 per ha for farm forestry;
- the opportunity cost of the farm land occupied by trees, taken to be proportional to the area taken up by trees – 12 per cent for shelterbelts, 2 per cent for farm forestry;
- other farm forestry costs of setting up seedling nurseries, distribution facilities and an extension network.

(continued on next page)

(continued)

For shelterbelts, a base case Internal Rate of Return of about 15 per cent was estimated. Sensitivity analysis on yield, costs, and underlying erosion produced a range of 13-17 per cent, while a consideration of the wood benefits only showed an IRR of 4.7 per cent. The base case for the farm forestry programme was an IRR of 19 per cent, with a range of 15-22 per cent in the sensitivity tests. The IRR for wood and fruit benefits only was 7.4 per cent.

The time profile of net benefits is significant. After year 17 net farmer income without the shelterbelt programme declined to zero and it is assumed that land is abandoned at this point. It is also noteworthy that for the first nine years of the shelterbelt programme gross farmer income with the project trails behind that "without", because of the effect of taking land out of production to plant the trees.

appearance of benefits. The justification is based on adding benefits previously left out of account, rather than applying an artificially low discount rate. Merely considering wood benefits would not justify proceeding with the scheme.

The results depend on assumptions which are sensitive to local conditions and project parameters, and which cannot be uncritically transferred from elsewhere. The assumption about the declining trend in soil fertility (0-2 per cent p.a.) without the project is also crucial, and awaits empirical confirmation. Nevertheless, the assumptions appear reasonable, and indicate what kind of information needs to collected for appraisal, and monitored on existing schemes of this kind.

The project has been underway for some time, and experience indicates that farmers' involvement in both components has been variable, despite the sound overall rate of return. This indicates the importance in appraisals of this kind to consider the distribution of both costs and benefits. Social and national net benefits should be reflected in sufficiently powerful incentives to the private agents involved — the farmers — to assure their enthusiastic involvement. If there is a mismatch between national and private gains, there is a case for adjusting private incentives, or rethinking the design of the project.

vi) *Replacing soil nutrients*

Intensive cultivation may exhaust soil fertility if it is not accompanied by the use of organic or chemical fertiliser, fallowing, rotation with legumes, or other standard means of husbanding the soil. Certain crops (cotton, maize, etc.) tend

Box 5.6.   **Case Study: Soil Erosion in Zimbabwe (Norse and Saigal, 1993)**

An intensive erosion research programme in Zimbabwe was instituted during the period of the Federation of Rhodesia and Nyasaland between the years 1953 and 1964. The data base is drawn from this source and covers 400 plot years of experiments conducted at the Henderson Research Station. A new model of soil loss estimation, SLEMSA (a modification of the Universal Soil Loss Equation) was constructed for the specific field conditions of Zimbabwe.

The raw data consisted of sludge measurements taken from the collecting tanks on the erosion plots. This gave records of nutrient concentration in percent for nitrogen (N) and organic carbon, and parts per million for phosphorous (P). These three nutrients represent the major quantitative impact of erosion on soil chemistry. Predictions were made of the losses of nutrients under given levels of erosion on different kinds of plots, and the cost of replacing these nutrients estimated from current market prices.

Soil loss was found to be correlated with losses of nitrogen, phosphorus, and organic carbon from experimental plots. In turn, variations in losses of soil nitrogen, organic carbon, and phosphorus were dependent on soil type, crop, and year. The two most important variables in explaining this effect were the rainfall pattern and the crop type. It was discovered that erosion is selective in removing nutrients from the soil. The ratios were highest in areas where run-off was highest, an important finding in evaluating physical conservation measures that are designed to detain soil but allow run-off. Specifically, it was found:

- on average, 1.6 million tons of nitrogen, 156 million tons of organic matter, and 0.24 million tons of phosphorus are lost annually by erosion. The arable lands alone lose 0.15, 1.5, and 0.02 million tons respectively;
- these nitrogen and phosphorus losses from arable land were about three times the level of total fertilizer application in Zimbabwe in the 1984-85 season, and they do not include losses of nutrients dissolved as runoff water;
- the equivalent cost of fertilizer containing these nutrients would have been US$1.5 billion per year (at 1985 market fertilizer prices and rates of exchange). For the arable lands alone, where there is the greatest investment in terms of food production and fertilizers, the financial cost amounted to US$150 million;
- on an annual per hectare basis, the financial cost of erosion was found to vary from US$20 to $50 on arable lands, and US$10 to $80 on grazing lands, according to the level of erosion;
- if the cost of replacing nutrients amounted to US$50 per hectare this would represent between 13 per cent to 60 per cent of the gross returns per hectare of arable land under maize production;
- the costs of soil erosion from arable land alone in Zimbabwe could exceed 16 per cent of agricultural GDP and 3 per cent of total GDP.

to be more demanding of soil fertility than others. Without measures consciously to restore soil fertility, the growth of crops depreciates the land's productive capacity, just as the use of a machine would reduce its value if it were not properly repaired and maintained.

The true measure of this "depreciation" of land would be the (capitalised) value of the future decline in yields. Since this could only be measured over a period of years in experimental conditions, an alternative approach is increasingly used. The consumption of different soil nutrients by the crop is measured by experiments, and the cost of replacing these by applying artificial fertiliser is estimated. It is acknowledged that the use of chemical fertiliser will not fully replace soil fertility – it will not compensate for the loss of minor, but crucial, trace elements, nor will it do anything for soil structure, for which animal or vegetable manures are required.

In short, the approach uses the technique of replacement cost to estimate the potential environmental damage of intensive cropping with insufficient fertilisation. For the reason mentioned above, it only provides minimum estimates of the true cost. Box 5.6. illustrates the approach.

Points to note from the case study

This exercise is typical of an increasing number of studies on the sustainability of farming systems, leading to estimates of the national cost of soil erosion and soil depletion. Such evidence underpins the growth of natural resource accounting, which seeks to incorporate environmental "depreciation" into conventional national accounting.

The data is derived from substantial agronomic fieldwork carried out in the country concerned. In some other cases (*e.g.* Mali) erosion data was transferred from neighbouring countries or other representative situations.

The cost of replacing nutrients understates the full cost of soil erosion and depletion. Other costs left out are those of soil crusting and compaction, acidification, declining response to fertilizer, reduced availability of soil moisture, greater competition from weeds, etc.

Off-site damages are also ignored, *e.g.* siltation of irrigation channels and reservoirs, effects on navigation and fisheries. On the other hand, erosion also redistributes soil within a catchment, and some farmers will benefit from soil accretion.

Replacement cost is one of several possible approaches to the cost of soil erosion. Others include the impact on production (dose-response) obtained from field trials correlating erosion with crop yield, and defensive expenditure data obtained from observing farmers' behaviour.

5.6. Problems and Limitations of MVPE

Following the above review of six applications of the MVPE method, it is time to draw some overall conclusions about the value of this approach, starting with some common problems.

Although the method seems very straightforward, the user should be aware of its limitations:

- The link between cause and effect is rarely as simple as it may seem. The physical relationships between the causes of environmental change, its symptoms, and its economic effects on output and costs are often quite elusive. Forging the link between cause and effect usually depends on making assumptions, transferring data on relationships established elsewhere, or taking an eclectic approach drawing evidence from a number of methods and sources.

- An observed change in the environment may be due to one or more of several causes, and it is often difficult to disentangle the effect of one cause from that of others. This is most clearly true of air pollution, which normally arises from a number of sources. Distinguishing the effect of human-made from natural degradation is also difficult (*e.g.* for erosion and acid rain damage to crops and trees).

- Where environmental change has a sizeable effect on markets, a more complex view needs to be taken of the market structure, elasticities, and supply and demand responses. Consumer behaviour needs to be introduced into the analysis.

- Determining cause and effect entails some assumption about what would have happened in the absence of a specific environmental change – setting up a "with" and "without" scenario. Unless this is done, there is a risk of attributing too much (or too little) damage to a particular cause. The problem arises where the event in question occurs in an ongoing process (*e.g.* where there is already serious air and water pollution or soil erosion).

- Prices, even when they are taken from an efficient and undistorted market, will underestimate economic values where there is significant consumers' surplus (Chapter 2). Market prices also exclude externalities, both positive and negative (Chapter 1).

5.7. Overall Evaluation of the MVPE Method

MVPE is the most widely used and intelligible valuation technique. Most valuation studies, especially in developing countries, rely upon it wholly or in part. It relies on observed market behaviour, is readily intelligible to decision-makers, and concentrates on output which potentially enters GNP and the budgets of firms and households. Its limitations are exposed where markets are badly developed or distorted, and where the changes in output are likely to have a significant effect on prices. Market prices also understate real economic values where consumer surpluses exist, and omit externalities.

Two reservations need to be made about the use of the method in developing or emerging market countries:

- Cause and effect relationships which have been established in temperate or high-income economies may not apply in different situations, *e.g.* the tropics. For instance, much of the work on the link between soil erosion and crop yields, or between shelterbelts and crop yields, or models of fish populations, has been done in temperate conditions. Almost all the dose-response relationships between air pollution and materials corrosion – which themselves are weak – have arisen from work in OECD countries and make no allowance for tropical climate, humidity, nor the very different range of materials at risk.

- Markets for some products are absent or underdeveloped, especially in subsistence economies. Recourse has to be made to roundabout valuation methods, or the use of proxies and substitutes.

Further References and Sources

DIXON *et al.* (1994) and Winpenny (1991) discuss the MVPE method in some detail, with many examples. Freeman (1993) and Desaigues et Point (1994) discuss some of the theoretical aspects.

The sources of the case material presented in this chapter are as follows:

BISHOP, Joshua and ALLEN, Jennifer, *The on-site costs of soil erosion in Mali*, World Bank Environment Department Working Paper, No. 21, Washington DC, 1989.

OSTRO, the report on which the case study of air pollution and health in Jakarta is based, is summarised in DIXON *et al.* (1994).

AUDIBERT, Martine, "Agricultural non-wage production and health status", *Journal of Development Economics*, 24, 1986.

MAGRATH, the report which is the source of the material on the Yellow River Basin of China, is summarised in DIXON *et al.*, 1994.

ANDERSON, Dennis, *The economics of afforestation: a case study in Africa*, World Bank Occasional Paper, World Bank/Johns Hopkins University Press, 1987.

NORSE, David and SAIGAL, Reshma, "National economic cost of soil erosion in Zimbabwe", in Mohan Munasinghe (ed.), *Environmental economics and natural resource management in developing countries*, World Bank/CIDIE, Washington DC, 1993.

Other references in this chapter are:

REPETTO, Robert, *et al.*, *Wasting assets: natural resources in the national income accounts*, World Resources Institute, Washington DC, 1989.

FAETH, Paul, *et al.*, *Paying the farm bill: US agricultural policy and the transition to sustainable agriculture*, World Resources Institute, Washington DC, 1991.

Chapter 6

SURVEY METHODS: CONTINGENT VALUATION

The previous chapter dealt with values obtained from applying market prices to physical environmental impacts. However, certain kinds of environmental changes do not affect goods and services that are marketed. For certain purposes, it is useful to know the total value of an elephant (apart from its meat, hide and ivory) or a whale (in addition to its meat and oil) – but there are no markets for these other attributes. Building a power station may destroy an attractive landscape and ruin the pleasure of ramblers: how can these effects be valued in the absence of a market for amenity and good views?

Contingent valuation (CV) can help in such situations. CV is a form of market research, where the good in question is a change in the environment:

- CV differs from conventional market research (*e.g.* for a new soap powder) in that it is concerned with a hypothetical event, namely an improvement or deterioration in the environment.

- CV often deals with changes in *public* goods – such as air quality, landscape, or the existence values of wildlife. However, it may also apply to environmental goods that are sold to individuals, such as improved water supply and sewerage.

- CV may apply both to *use* values (*e.g.* water quality, viewing wild animals, direct enjoyment of a view) or *non-use* values (existence values).

- The values that people express in CV interviews depend (are **contingent**) upon such factors as the description of the good, whether it is provided, and the way it would be paid for.

CV has great potential as a source of data in areas where other techniques are not feasible, or as a check on data obtained by other methods. It is increasingly common to find CV being used in combination with other techniques. The method has recently made great strides with the help of advances in scientific sampling

---

Box 6.1. **Value of Kenya's Parks and Reserves**

Contingent valuation surveys have been used to provide estimates of the value of Kenya's parks and reserves. The context for this work is the controversy over the value of keeping large areas of land devoted to wildlife and the preservation of natural habitat. It has been argued that the opportunity cost of conserving biodiversity, in the sense of the profits of agricultural and livestock production which is foregone because of current land use, is in the region of US$192 million per annum (Norton-Griffiths, 1993). This is much greater than the net profits attributable to wildlife tourism and forestry activities in the parks and reserves, estimated to be US$42 million. It is difficult to persuade communities adjacent to parks and reserves, some of whom have claims on the land, of the benefits of continuing to use the land in this way.

However, willingness-to-pay surveys uncovered a considerable consumer surplus amongst tourists to Kenya's parks and reserves, compared to what they were actually paying at present. This implies that they would be prepared to pay much more than at present for their own enjoyment of the wildlife (use values) as well as for the knowledge that the wildlife would continue to exist (existence values). The size of the consumer surplus was estimated to be $248 million annually (central estimate) which indicates the scale of the benefit provided from the continued protection of these areas, and the scope for raising charges and extracting more revenue from this sector. These benefits exceed the opportunity cost of the land, quoted above.

There is an asymmetry between the distribution of costs and benefits from the parks and reserves. The costs (mainly opportunity costs, but also damage to houses and crops from wild animals) fall mainly on local people, while the benefits identified in the CV survey accrue mainly to foreign visitors and other nature lovers. This indicates the need for redistributing income from conservation in favour of local people. It also provides a strong rationale for international subvention of Kenya's efforts to protect biodiversity, through such means as the Global Environment Facility.

Source: Moran, 1994.

---

theory, the economic theory of benefit estimation, computerised data management, and public opinion polling. It can have important feed-back into policy formation (Box 6.1). The use of CV in the USA received a powerful impetus from the extensive litigation in the aftermath of the Exxon Valdez oil spillage in Alaska, where the issue was how to value the damage to the landscape and wildlife.

Its principal drawback is that it depends on what people **say** rather than what they **do** – although there are methods which help to compensate for the various biases that arise. Obtaining reliable information requires a substantial investment of time, care and resources, which makes a good CV exercise expensive.

This chapter introduces the reader to:

- subject areas for which CV is appropriate;
- the overall structure of a CV study;
- biases and problems that arise and how they can be overcome;
- how the data can be analysed;
- guidelines for conducting a CV.

The discussion is illustrated from an actual case drawn from a Caribbean country.

6.1. When is CV Appropriate?

CV is potentially useful for the following types of problem or sector:

- air and water quality;
- recreation (including fishing, hunting, parks, wildlife);
- conservation of unpriced natural assets such as forests and wilderness areas;
- option and existence values of biodiversity;
- risks to life and health;
- transport improvements;
- water, sanitation and sewerage.

CV is appropriate where:

- environmental changes have no direct impact on marketed output;
- it is not feasible to observe peoples' preferences directly;
- the population in the sample is representative, interested in and well informed of the subject in question;
- there are adequate funds, human resources and time to do a proper study.

6.2. Overall Structure of a CV Study

CV surveys ask respondents questions about values they place on environmental change. Typical questions would include: "Would you be willing to pay $x to [improve air/water quality, preserve views of an attractive landscape, improve coastal waters to swimmable standards, etc.]? Would you connect to a public water supply/ sewerage system if standards of service improved, and if so, how much per month would you be willing to pay?"

Three of the fundamental decisions to be made concern the type of interview, the design of the questionnaire, and the way the questions are posed (elicitation procedure).

Interviews can be carried out by mail, telephone or by personal visits. The best results can be expected from personal interviews, provided the enumerators are capable and well-trained. In countries with limited telephone ownership, poor postal services and widespread illiteracy, personal interviews will be the only realistic choice. Personal interviews are, on the other hand, relatively expensive, and the enumerators need to be well-trained.

Where telephones are in widespread use, telephone interviews offer the advantage of cheapness, economy of time, and the ease of obtaining a representative sample though random dialling methods. However, there are limits to how much information can be conveyed by this method, and people are unwilling to spend very long on the telephone.

Mail surveys are cheap and avoid biases caused by the quality of the enumerator. They depend on good postal services and a good general level of literacy. However, mail surveys usually have low response rates, and only people interested in the topic will bother to reply. Also, it is impossible to control the order in which questions are answered.

In practice, combinations of the three types of interview are possible, *e.g.* a mail survey followed up by telephone or personal calls.

The **design of the questionnaire** is of critical importance. It should normally begin with an account of the problem, *e.g.* the environmental change that is envisaged, illustrated if possible with diagrams or photographs. This is to ensure that the respondent is aware of the issue and well-informed about it.

Where environmental improvements (*e.g.* water supply, sewerage) are the subject of the survey, the interview should convey information on when the service would be available, how the respondent would be expected to pay for it, how much others would be expected to pay, what the modalities of delivery of the service would be, and its quality and reliability.

The second part of the questionnaire should elicit the value that the respondent would place on the environmental change. For environmental improvements, questions should be designed to uncover **willingness to pay** (WTP). For losses to the environment, the respondents should in theory be asked about their **willingness to accept** (WTA) compensation. Surveys in which both WTP and WTA measures are used regularly show a significant difference between the two answers, and in practice WTP tends to be used. Typically, WTA is several times larger than WTP, which reflects the fact that WTA is not limited by income, and most people place a higher value on what they already have than on something they may hypothetically acquire.

Thirdly, the questionnaire should include a set of questions about the social, economic and demographic background of the respondents and their families. This information is necessary to analyse and cross-check their WTP replies, especially where the answers are of a yes/no nature (see below).

There are two main types of *elicitation procedure*. People could be asked the most they would be willing to pay, or the least they would accept in compensation, for the change in question. These are called **direct** or **open-ended** questions. An alternative is to ask whether they would be prepared to buy the service or accept the change if it cost a specified amount (a **yes/no or dichotomous question**). The latter has the advantage of avoiding certain biases in answers (see below). It also has the advantage of mimicking the decisions of consumers buying goods at a fixed price, or when they vote for certain public programmes with a specific cost attached, as in many US states and Switzerland. However, the dichotomous type of question demands more complex statistical treatment and some strict assumptions to come up with maximum WTP. Other variants are possible, such as asking yes/no questions for a range of prices to discover threshold levels for each informant, and asking the respondent to use payment cards or "Monopoly money" to facilitate replies to open-ended questions.

The annex to this chapter contains the format of one actual CV questionnaire.

6.3. Analysing the Data

CV studies may contain three levels of analysis of respondents' data.

- Firstly, a frequency distribution is drawn up, relating the size of different WTP statements to the number of people making them.
- Secondly, WTP responses are cross-tabulated with the respondents' socio-economic characteristics and other relevant factors.
- Thirdly, multivariate statistical techniques are employed to correlate answers to the respondents' socioeconomic attributes.

The simplest kind of CV **elicitation procedure** is the open-ended question about WTP. For each price, the total amount of WTP is added, and a demand curve can be built up from these data. This shows how the demand, or WTP, for the environmental change varies with its "price". Carrying out the second of the above procedures should be done as a useful check on the plausibility of the answers.

For CV studies using yes/no questions (the **referendum model)** the second and third of the above steps will be necessary to produce a valuation or demand function. The result is either a probability-weighted distribution of WTP various amounts among the sample population, or an estimate of the proportion of the population WTP a particular amount. **Discrete choice** statistical methods are used to process the data.

In any event, a preliminary screening, or **cleaning**, of the data should be conducted to remove suspect answers, protest replies, or outliers. This should be done with care, to reduce the risk of the analyst injecting his or her own biases or expectations into the data sample. However, note should be taken of extreme WTP answers, such as zero replies, and their true significance established, if possible.

Grossing up estimates obtained from samples is a common statistical problem, which can be eased by the careful choice of random samples. The involvement of a professional statistician with sampling experience is highly desirable, particularly in deciding on sampling methods and sample sizes. Another type of sampling problem is the treatment of **non-responses**, especially where this is suspected to be non-random. A high proportion of non-responses may signify a problem; for certain types of survey this may be normal, but for others it may indicate a problem with the method. In yes/no elicitation procedures there should also be room for a "no reply" answer, with a follow up question on the reasons for this choice.

The careful definition of target population is important and can obviously affect the size of society's aggregate WTP. This is a key problem for environmental issues of national or even international importance where there are many potential **stakeholders**.

Once the analysis has been done, it is desirable to carry out tests of the reliability of the data and the methodology. The three main types of check are as follows:

i) Internal checks on survey design, by varying certain details between different split-samples to see whether systematic differences arise. The following design details may need to be checked by the use of focus groups: starting points for WTP bids; elicitation procedures, especially the open-ended versus yes/no approaches; effects of "time to think"; the order of questions; and the amount of information provided.

ii) Multivariate analysis, correlating WTP with socioeconomic variables suggested by demand theory (*e.g.* income, education, family status, housing conditions, etc.). If the correlations do not follow a predictable pattern, this would be *prima facie* reason to question the survey methods.

iii) Comparison of the CV valuations with those obtained from other methods, where these are available and appropriate. It may also be possible to compare what people said they would be willing to pay with what they actually paid, where a scheme has been in operation for sufficient time. If there is a reasonable correspondence between estimates obtained from different methods, this is reassuring. However, if there is not, this is not necessarily a condemnation of the CV results, since other methods are likely to have their problems and biases. In this case, a more complex judgement needs to be made about the relative accuracy of estimates obtained by CV and other methods.

6.4. Common Problems, and How to Deal with Them

Some answers may be misleading because they are casual or frivolous, others may mislead because of deliberate or unconscious biases.

The likelihood of ignorant or flippant answers can be reduced by offering respondents proper information about the proposed change, including graphics and photographs. Sometimes it would be beneficial to offer more time to answer, for instance by returning the following day to complete the interview. How much information to provide is a judicious decision: providing too much data may itself be a source of bias, which ideally should be tested by comparing the answers of the sample with a control group being offered less information. At the very least, all respondents within a sample should be offered the same information, and interviewers should be sparing in the amount of supplementary information they volunteer in response to questions.

It may be necessary to identify clearly implausible replies (**outliers**, in statistical terms) and eliminate them from the sample (to produce **trimmed means**).

Another kind of innocent bias may arise from the respondents' misunderstanding of the nature of the enquiry. This may be due either to insufficient background information, or from bad communication between the enumerator and the respondent. One common error is for the respondent to confuse the subject of the enquiry with other, wider, questions that the subject arouses in his or her mind. This is referred to as the **embedding** problem, alternatively as the **part/whole** bias.

If, for example, people are asked their WTP for the preservation of a particular natural habitat, their answers may betray their values for the whole of that natural habitat in the country (or even in the world, in the case of threatened species). The only safeguard against this bias is for the background information to be clear that the questions relate solely to the case in point.

It is important to avoid any hint or cue, in the questions or the manner of the interviewer, about the level of WTP values that are expected. If, for instance, people are questioned about their WTP for an ascending, or descending, range of values, their answers may be influenced by the starting level (**starting point bias**). The same problem may arise from the use of payment cards with different levels of value on them, or from using bidding games. In the interest of objectivity, respondents should be discouraged from guessing what level of WTP they are expected to produce, or the average level of other peoples' replies.

WTP replies may be biased by the choice of **payment vehicle** specified in the question, *e.g.* a cash price, entry charge, indirect tax, property tax supplement, voluntary donation, once-and-for-all or recurrent charge, etc. This is referred to as **instrument bias**. On the other hand, the "bias" between various forms of payment may reflect peoples' genuine preferences, in which case they should not be disregarded or corrected for. In the case of a service that might actually be introduced (*e.g.* improved household water supplies) the payment method specified in the CV questionnaire should be as realistic as possible.

Deliberate bias may arise where the informants understate their true preference for a good, or exaggerate the amount of compensation they would really need. One obvious motive would be to "free ride" on the provision of public amenities, that is, to hope to benefit from public provision without contributing to it. Alternatively, people may try to get away with paying less than the change is really worth to them. This is known as **strategic bias**. Another motive would be to use the survey to register a protest at the idea of a charge for something they would expect to enjoy free (a **protest response**).

One common way of countering strategic bias is to ask respondents a "yes/no" question about whether they would be willing to pay a particular sum. The sample is split into different groups (**split-samples**), each being asked whether they would be WTP a single sum, this sum being different for each group. This was the approach used in the case study reported below in this chapter. The sums concerned should obviously be chosen with care, so that potential free-riders are discouraged from giving misleading negative answers. The upper and lower bound values should be pretested so that, for WTP questions, the upper level would produce almost 100 per cent rejection, while the lower one would elicit almost 100 per cent acceptance. The different WTP values are then distributed randomly across the split-samples.

Box 6.2. **Guidelines for Using CVM (Arrow *et al.*, 1993)**

The following desiderata, amongst others, were produced in a report of the Contingent Valuation Panel, co-chaired by Kenneth Arrow and Robert Solow, to the US National Oceanic and Atmospheric Administration in the aftermath of the Exxon Valdez oil spill in Alaska.

The guidelines apply to estimating non-use values of natural habitats. In the USA, evidence of damage to the non-use values of natural resources is admissible in the award of damages to trustees and others. Hence the CVM is becoming widely used in litigation, and substantial resources are being made available for the conduct of CV studies. This should be borne in mind in reading the guidelines below, not all of which may be appropriate in their full rigour for applications in other countries, or for other purposes.

Sample. A professional statistician should be involved in the choice of the type and size of the sample. The sample size must be statistically significant, especially where split-samples are used.

Non-responses. A high non-response rate would make the survey results unreliable.

Interviews. Face-to-face interviews are usually preferable to other types, and telephone interviews are better than mail surveys. Major CV surveys should also pretest for the effect of the interviewer. The effects of photographs on the respondents should be carefully explored.

Reporting. The survey report should contain information on the population sampled, the sampling frame used, sample size, the overall non-response rate and breakdown of non-responses, a copy of the questionnaire, and all communications with respondents. Data should be archived and accessible to interested parties.

Questionnaire design. Questionnaires should be piloted and pre-tested. There should be evidence that respondents understand and accept the description and questions in it. In general, the structure of the survey should err on the conservative side, i.e. options which underestimate WTP should be preferred to those which risk overestimating it, in order to improve the credibility of results. There should be a place for "no-answers", the reasons for which should be explored.

Cross-tabulations. The survey should include a variety of other questions that help to interpret replies to the primary valuation question. These might include income and other socio-economic indicators, location, awareness of environmental issues, etc.

Elicitation procedure. The WTP format is preferable to questions about compensation required. The valuation questions should be posed as a vote on a referendum ("yes/no", rather than an open ended question about WTP). The mode of payment should be clear, realistic and acceptable.

Accurate description of issue. Sufficient information should be provided about the environmental issue in question, and about what remedy is being offered. Respondents should be reminded of the existence of substitute commodities or other comparable natural resources.

Expenditure implications. Respondents should be reminded that their WTP for the programme in question would reduce their ability to spend on other goods and services.

Other precautions against strategic bias can be taken. Respondents should **not** be told that payment by others would be compulsory, but should be told that the provision of the service would depend on a demonstration of adequate WTP. They could be briefed that if they exaggerated the amount they would be WTP they may not be able to afford it if that amount were really charged. Conversely, if WTP were understated, the service might not be provided, which would also be an undesired outcome.

A considerable body of experience of conducting CVs has now been accumulated, and practitioners have started to formulate guidelines of "good practice". Box 6.2 contains desiderata formulated by an authoritative panel concerned with non-use values used in litigation following damage to natural resources. It should be noted that most of this experience has been acquired in developed countries, where respondents are familiar with questionnaire surveys and knowledgeable about the environmental issues being raised. Most people in developing countries lack such a background, and CVs have proved more useful for issues of direct everyday relevance (especially water and sanitation) than for more abstract or remote issues (*e.g.* biodiversity).

Many of the issues discussed in this chapter were considered and resolved in the case study outlined in Box 6.3.

Points to note from the case study

- the issue – sewerage – was well understood by the respondents and concerned a use value within their direct experience;
- a realistic mode of payment was proposed;
- the referendum mode (yes/no) was used to reduce the likelihood of strategic bias;
- a range of other questions was included to discover respondents' other characteristics;
- split samples were used to test the effect of different WTP levels;
- a logic function was used for the econometric benefit estimation.

However,

- the description of the proposed environmental improvement is vague, and could have been improved by the use of photographs and maps. Moreover, uncertainty is introduced by stating that the pollution *might* affect tourism and *can* damage coral reefs. People's WTP could depend on their subjective interpretation of the probability of this happening;

- respondents could have been reminded of their budget constraint, as well as the other public goods they could spend money on.

Box 6.3.   **Case Study: A Public Sewerage Project in the Caribbean**

The public sewerage project under analysis is designed to run parallel to a densely populated beach area on a Caribbean island whose primary foreign exchange earnings are from tourism services. The service area includes commercial (including hotels), residential, and institutional users. At present, the island's citizens provide their own sanitary services. The majority have wells that allow excreta to filter slowly through the limestone formation to the sea. There are some septic systems and a few package treatment plants.

In general, the population of the potential service area is fairly satisfied with the existing system. The government fears, however, that the filtration of excreta into the coastal waters may be having serious consequences. It is believed that filtration of sewage may be damaging the fringing reefs: *a)* which are important to the food chain of the fishing industry and *b)* which help protect against beach erosion. More importantly, the government fears that continued filtration of sewage will make the waters unsafe for swimming by nationals and will cause tourism to decline.

The results of a previous sewerage project in the country suggested that willingness to pay of private users was not sufficient to cover the costs of the project. In that previous case, potential users preferred to continue to use their own facilities rather than pay the connection fee and the costs to adapt their plumbing to use the public system. There was reason to believe, however, that significant benefits might be received by people who would not be connected to the system, and that it was worth analysing the project.

The typical interview contained three parts (see Annex):

* A detailed description of the good being valued and the hypothetical circumstance under which it would be made available to the respondent.
* Questions which elicited the respondent's willingness to pay for the good.
* Questions about the respondent's characteristics, preferences, and uses of the goods being valued.

The valuation questions were asked in a dichotomous (yes/no) format – for example: Would you be willing to pay $15 more on your water bill each quarter to have public sewerage or would you prefer to pay what you are now paying and go without the public sewerage system?

It is well known that the form, wording, order, and context of a questionnaire can affect the answers received in unexpected ways. The concepts and questions were therefore investigated with focus groups and a pilot survey. Focus groups are discussion groups comprised of people selected from the population of potential beneficiaries and led by someone familiar with market research and social psychology. Their objective is to learn how respondents conceptualize and talk about the topics being investigated. Focus groups are used to explore hypotheses and to formulate specific questions for quantitative research. Often the vocabulary used in the discussion is adopted to phrase the questionnaire.

(continued on next page)

(continued)

The final CV survey covered 277 households that would be connected to the sewerage system and 433 households that lived outside the area to be connected to the sewerage system but used the beaches that would be affected by the project. The total population of these two areas was 3 268 and 53 041 households, respectively.

A different questionnaire was used in each area. Households who lived outside the sewer district were asked only about the environmental benefits of the sewer system. They were offered two choices: pay a certain dollar amount in their quarterly water bill for the construction and maintenance of the sewer system, or not pay and not receive the corresponding services.

The specific dollar amounts that a respondent was asked about were assigned to the questionnaires on a random basis. For the households located in the area to be connected to the sewer system, the proposed method of payment was a sewerage charge that would cover both the services of the public sewerage system and cleaner beaches.

Households were told the potential impact of disposing of wastewater into the ground, and the potential for avoiding beach pollution and damaged reefs by construction of the sewer system. The interviewer also used an illustration (see Annex 4A) to reinforce the differences between the situation with and without the project.

The use of closed-end questions ("yes or no" to a specific dollar amount) made it impossible to determine directly the willingness-to-pay. Therefore, the willingness-to-pay responses had to be transformed into benefit estimates. To do this, we exercised the standard practice of using an econometric model to relate the probability of a "yes" response to the amount of payment and household characteristics to obtain mean values for the sample's willingness to pay. The exogenous variables used were: whether the respondent used the beaches, the respondent's age, whether the respondent saw the television coverage about beach pollution, and the amount of the randomly assigned sewer charge. All of the coefficients estimated were significant at the 95 percent level.

The estimates of mean willingness-to-pay were US$178 and US$11 per year for households inside and outside the area to be connected, respectively. The larger mean benefit derived for the catchment households captured both the private and public benefit while the smaller mean benefits derived for the outside catchment households measured only environmental or public benefits.

A second problem with the CV question was that it did not specify when the water would become unswimmable. It merely specified that it would eventually become unfit for swimming. In addition, there was no information on the views of the respondents on how contaminated the waters were or what their implicit time frame was. Clearly the perceived immediacy of the problem should have some impact on the amount people would be willing to pay to solve it.

Source: Darling, Gomez and Niklitschek, 1992.

6.5. Overall Evaluation of CV

CV is a technique with great potential utility, but which needs very careful stag-ing and interpretation. It is very data-intensive, and the proper conduct of surveys is costly and time-consuming. The design of surveys and interpretation of their responses has become a specialised activity.

CV is applicable to problems and circumstances that fall outside the scope of other methods, which accounts for its popularity. In practice, most of the empirical work has been done on air and water quality, amenity, conservation, and existence values. In developing countries it is producing important evidence on willingness-to-pay in the water and sanitation sector.

Its greatest weakness is that it relies on peoples' views, rather than evidence of their market behaviour. Many possible biases may arise in responses, but some of these can be controlled – if not eliminated – by ingenious survey design. CV relies on the respondents understanding the environmental issue at stake, and its likely impact on them. This assumes a certain level of education and environmental aware-ness. These conditions are more likely to be satisfied for urgent local concerns than for national or global issues.

Box 6.4 contains the conclusions of a recent high-level assessment of the CV method.

Box 6.4. **Conclusions of the NOAA Panel on Contingent Valuation**

"It has been argued in the literature and in comments addressed to the Panel that the results of CV studies are variable, sensitive to details of the survey instrument used, and vulnerable to upward bias. These arguments are plausible. However, some antagonists of the CV approach go so far as to suggest that there can be no useful information content to CV results. The Panel is unpersuaded by these extreme arguments.

[earlier in the report] we identify a number of stringent guidelines for the conduct of CV studies. These require that respondents be carefully informed about the particular en-vironmental damage to be valued, and about the full extent of substitutes and undamaged alternatives available. In willingness-to-pay scenarios, the payment vehicle must be pre-sented fully and clearly, with the relevant budget constraint emphasised. The payment scenario should be convincingly described, preferably in a referendum context, because most respondents will have had experience with referendum ballots with less than perfect background information. Where choices in formulating the CV instrument can be made, we urge they lean in the conservative direction, as a partial or total offset to the likely tendency to exaggerate willingness to pay."

Source: Arrow, Solow *et al.*, Report of NOAA Panel, 1993.

Further References and Sources

One of the best recent texts on contingent valuation is: Mitchell, Robert C. and Carson, Robert T., *Using surveys to value public goods; the contingent valuation method*, Resources for the Future, Washington DC, 1989.

There is a balanced discussion of CV in the *Journal of Economic Perspectives*, Fall, 8(4), 1994, summed up in the article by Paul Portney, "The contingent valuation debate: why economists should care".

Other references used in this chapter are as follows:

MORAN, Dominic, "Contingent valuation and biodiversity: measuring the user surplus of Kenyan protected areas", *Biodiversity and Conservation*, 3, 1994.

DARLING, Arthur H., GOMEZ, Christian and NIKLITSCHEK, Mario E., "The question of a public sewerage system in a Caribbean country: a case study", in Munasinghe, Mohan (ed.), *Environmental economics and natural resource management in developing countries*, World Bank/CIDIE, Washington DC, 1993.

NORTON-GRIFFITHS, M., "The opportunity costs of biodiversity conservation in Kenya", a paper from the Centre for Social and Economic Research on the Global Environment (CSERGE), London WC1E 6BT, 1993.

Annex

QUESTIONNAIRE SURVEY
OF HOUSEHOLD CONNECTIONS
TO PUBLIC SEWERAGE

1. Preamble

Good morning/afternoon. The Department of Health is conducting a survey on the feasibility of installing a public sewer system in this community. The interview will take just a few minutes, and your views are important for the study. Yours answers are confidential. Before I start, may I ask how long you have lived in this house?

2. Preamble to CV Question

Currently much of the community's waste water goes into the ground. This water drains through the ground into the ocean. The wastes in this water will eventually contaminate the beach water, making it unfit for swimming. This contaminated or polluted beach water might also discourage tourism to our island. There is also a possibility that polluted ocean water can damage some of the coral reefs.

2.1. *How important are clean beaches to you?*

1. Very important   ❑

2. Important   ❑

3. Not important   ❑

2.2. Do you or members of your household visit beaches?

1. Never ☐

2. 1 to 15 times per year ☐

3. More than 15 times per year ☐

In order to keep beach water clean for swimming and to eliminate the potential threat to coral reefs, we need to build a central sewerage system. This system would collect waste and sewage water from households and establishment plant where it would be treated to remove damaging pollutants. It could then be discharged safely into the ocean far from the shore. However, this is expensive. Substantial construction is required. One way to pay for part of the system is with a quarterly sewerage charge covering hookup and continuing operating costs.

2.3. Which of the following would you choose?

1. Pay a quarterly sewer charges
of $... for public sewage disposal
and clean beaches ☐

2. Not pay the $... quarterly sewer
charge and continue
with the current system ☐

If yes, skip to 2.5.

**2.4. What was the main reason you said NO or would not answer?
(Ask and then categorise yourself)**

1. Does not use public beaches ☐

2. Does not want a higher water bill ☐

3. Can't afford it ☐

4. Wants to pay another way ☐

5. Not enough information ❏

6. Does not understand question ❏

7. Cannot decide ❏

8. Other ❏

2.5. If the government installed the house connection on your property during construction of the sewer system, would you be prepared to meet the cost of connecting by a long-term, low-interest loan?

1. Yes ❏

2. No ❏

2.6. By instalment added to your quarterly sewer rate?

1. Yes ❏

2. No ❏

2.7. If the public sewer system is constructed would you:

1. Connect with the system immediately ❏

2. Connect eventually ❏

3. Not connect to the system ❏

3. Identification of residence

3.1. Address

3.2. What is the tenancy of your residence? The dwelling is:

1. Owned   ❏

2. Rented/leased   ❏

3. Other   ❏

3.3. The land is:

1. Owned   ❏

2. Rented/leased   ❏

3. Other   ❏

3.4. Type of residence

1. Chattel   ❏

2. Blockwall   ❏

3. Wood and wall   ❏

3.5. Number of rooms _____

4.   Respondent characteristis

4.1. *Sex*

1. Male ☐

2. Female ☐

4.2. *Age* _____

4.3. *Does your work or that of members of your household depend directly on the business from tourists? Examples: taxis, restaurants, hotels*

1. Yes ☐

2. No ☐

4.4. *How many people live in your house?* _____

4.5. *How many people 18 or Over?* _____

4.6. *And what number best describes the total income of all persons in the household for 1990?*

Number _____

1. Less than $3 000

2. $3 001 to $5 000

3. $5 001 to $7 500

4. $7 501 to $10 000

5. $10 001 to $15 000

6. $15 001 to $25 000

7. $25 001 to $50 000

8. $50 001 to $75 000

9. More than $75 000

10. No response or don't know

4.7. Have you seen the recent TV coverage on the potential for marine pollution here on the island?

1. Yes ❏

2. No ❏

5.   Conditions of house

5.1. Is your water piped into your house?

1. Yes ❏

2. No ❏

If yes, skip to 5.3.

5.2. Into your yard?

1. Yes ❏

2. No ❏

5.3. Where does your sink and bath water drain (water from kitchen sink, laundry, and shower/bath)?

1. Sewage well   ❏

2. Septic tank   ❏

3. Garden   ❏

4. Street   ❏

5. Pit   ❏

6. Public drain   ❏

5.4. Where does the sewage from the toilet drain?

1. Sewage well   ❏

2. Septic tank   ❏

3. Pit toilet   ❏

5.5. Do you share toilet facilities with other households?

1. Yes   ❏

2. No   ❏

5.6. How long has the septic tank (pit or sewage) been in use?

1. 0 to 5 years   ❏

2. 6 to 10 years   ❏

3. More than 10 years   ❏

5.7. Have you had any problems with your sewage system in the last three years?

Problem	yes	no
1. Overflow	❑	❑
2. Flooding	❑	❑
3. Blocked	❑	❑
4. Other	❑	❑

5.8. Do you think you will have to replace your septic tank (*pit or sewage*) within the next year?

1. Yes   ❑

2. No   ❑

5.9. How much have you spent in the last year for operation and maintenance or repair of your sewage system?

Chapter 7

REVEALED PREFERENCES AND PROXY MARKETS

One of the underlying problems of environmental economics discussed in Chapter I is that of **missing markets** for environmental quality. The value of the environment cannot be discovered directly from the prices and quantities observed in environmental transactions. People do not buy and sell environmental quality directly.

However, peoples' preferences for the environment can be inferred indirectly by examining their behaviour in markets that are linked to the environment. Some goods and services are complements to environmental quality, others are proxies, surrogates or substitutes for it. By examining the prices they pay, or the benefits they apparently derive, in these closely-related markets, peoples' environmental preferences can be inferred.

Three principal techniques will be examined in this chapter:

- **Travel cost method (TCM)**, which uses the time and cost incurred in visiting and enjoying a natural site as a proxy for the price of entering it.

- **Avertive behaviour (AB)**, **defensive expenditure (DE)** take their cues from what people are observed to spend to protect themselves against an actual or potential decline in their environmental quality.

- **Hedonic pricing method (HPM)** relies on the notion that the price of a property reflects, amongst other things, the quality of the environment in which it is located. This value is unbundled from that of the various other factors making up the specific property price.

All three methods estimate people's **revealed preferences** from data on their **observed** market behaviour. In this respect they differ from the technique discussed in Chapter 6 which draws Information from peoples' **stated** preferences.

7.1. The Travel Cost Method

TCM comes into its own for the valuation of natural sites or environmental resources that are unpriced, in the sense that there is no entrance charge or other fee for users. The problem is then to find quantitative evidence of the value of these unpriced resources to visitors. One possibility is to ask them directly. This is the contingent valuation method, and was considered in Chapter 6. Another approach is to take the visitors' travel cost as a proxy for the "price" they are willing to pay.

The principle behind TCM is that, rather than pay an entrance, or service, fee, users incur direct transport costs, or outlay their own time, in order to make the visit. The usual assumption of economists is that less of a good is demanded as its price goes up. By analogy, the number of visits would normally be inversely related to the size of travel cost. The information on peoples' response to their travel costs is used to draw up a demand curve for the resource in question (as in Chapter 2), and the area under the curve is interpreted as the total benefit of the resource. The whole of this amount is consumers' surplus and, in theory, indicates the scope for levying charges on visitors, if that is feasible.

When is TCM appropriate?

TCM is potentially useful in the following situations or sectors:

- recreational sites (Box 7.1);
- nature reserves, national parks, forests and wetlands used for recreation;
- dams, reservoirs, forests, etc. with recreational by-products;
- fuelwood supply;
- collection of drinking water.

It is appropriate where:

- the site is accessible, for at least part of the time;
- there is no direct charge or entry fee for the good or service in question, or where such charges are very low;
- people expend significant time or other costs to travel to the site.

Procedure for deriving a demand curve

The main steps involved in TCM are:

Box 7.1.   **Recreational Values from Travel Cost Studies in the USA**

In a review of almost 300 TCM studies done in the USA between 1968 and 1988, it was found that the mean value for a recreation day, updated to 1987 prices, was US$34. The average benefit of different activities varied from $12 to $72 per day, with the highest values reported for hunting, fishing, nonmotorized boating, hiking and winter sports (Walsh, Johnson and McKean, 1992).

This study compared the unit values for the same activity produced by TCM and the contingent valuation method (CV – see Chapter 6). It was found that TCM values were typically 20-30 per cent higher than those produced by CV, mainly because TCM values the entire trip including both primary and secondary activities (*e.g.* fishing, swimming, picnicking) whereas CV usually values the primary activity alone (*e.g.* fishing).

- dividing the area into zones;
- sampling visitors to the site;
- obtaining visitation rates for each zone;
- estimating travel costs;
- obtaining a statistical regression;
- constructing a demand curve.

These are discussed below.

i)   *Zoning*

The area around the site is first divided into zones, such that the travel cost to the site from each point in the same zone is roughly equal. In the most straightforward cases the zones could be drawn using concentric circles around the site. But the zones could also be irregular contours, or even non-concentric, depending on how travel costs varied within the catchment area of the site. In a well-known TCM study in Bangkok, the zones correspond to different districts of the city (Grandstaff and Dixon, 1986). In the case study discussed below, the zones used are the national *cantons*.

Zoning becomes much more problematic if it is decided to include foreign visitors in the exercise, which may be justified in the case of an attraction of international standing (*e.g.* Victoria Falls, Grand Canyon, Antarctica, leading African game reserves). One simplification is to define zones according to their travel costs Instead of distance. The TCM method encounters fewer problems if it is conducted within a single country or region.

ii)   *Sampling visitors*

Questionnaire surveys are undertaken amongst visitors to the site. Data is collected on the characteristics of the visitor, the motives for the visit, travel costs, and attributes of the environmental resource. Specifically, information is collected on:

- number of visitors;
- place of origin;
- frequency of visit;
- socio-economic attributes;
- duration of journey, time spent at site;
- direct travel expenses;
- respondent's valuation of time;
- number of years that visits have been made;
- success, or otherwise, of previous hunting and fishing trips;
- total population in each zone;
- other motives for trip, other sites visited during the journey;
- environmental quality attributes of site and its substitutes.

The survey can be carried out at the site, on travel routes to it, in the households of visitors in the catchment area, or in a combination of these locations. The important thing is to get a representative sample.

iii)   *Visitation rates*

For each zone the number of annual visits (or visitor-days in the case of overnight stays) per head of the total population is estimated from the survey information.

iv)   *Travel cost estimation*

The main items to be costed are:

- direct expenses incurred by visitors in getting to and from the site, including fares, fuel and other incidentals;

- the value of time spent on the journey, including time spent at the site. Valuing leisure time is inherently problematic; most empirical attempts arrive at values of between one quarter and one half of the average prevailing wage rate. If there are no specific estimates of the value of leisure to hand, a yardstick of one-third average wages may be taken;

- entry fees, guide fees and other incidental expenses at the site;

For round trips involving several sites travel costs may need to be allocated between each site in a *pro rata* fashion.

v)   Statistical regression

The next step is to test the relationship between visitation rates and relevant explanatory factors. This is done through multiple regression analysis, which seeks to "explain" visitation rates in terms of travel costs, other socio-economic variables, and the prices and distances of competing sites. One typical functional form is given in Box 7.2.

Box 7.2.   **Typical Functional Form for TCM**

$Vi = a + bTCi + cINCi + dEDi + \ldots fSTCi,$

where V is the number of visits to the site, TC is the total travel cost, INC is the individual's income, ED is the respondent's educational level, STC is the travel cost to substitute sites, i is the respondent, and a, b, c, d, and f are the coefficients to be estimated. Coefficient b is of particular interest, denoting the change in visitation rate as a function of travel cost.

The choice of functional form determines the results obtained. There is some consensus that a **semi-log** form gives the best results, namely regressing the logarithm of visitation rate against travel cost, etc.

---

vi)   Constructing a demand curve

The object of the exercise is to produce a demand curve for the environmental resource in question. If people's visitation rate can be shown to vary according to the "price" they pay, for which their travel cost is a proxy, this relationship can be viewed as a "demand curve" for the environment.

Given a demand function relating visitation to travel cost, the final step is to "anchor" the data to the actual level of visits, and generate points on the demand curve by iteration. In Figure 7.1 the curve MA is built up starting at point A, the observed number of visits when the entry charge is zero. It is then assumed that visitors would react to the imposition an admission fee, and successive increases in it, in the same way as they are observed to respond to differences in their travel cost. Sites with unique or compelling features would tend to have relatively steep demand curves, implying that many visitors were prepared to travel long distances to get there. On the other hand, less interesting sites would have flatter demand curves, reflecting the unwillingness of visitors to travel far to them.

If a certain number of visits occurred at an entrance fee of zero, positive rising entrance fees would normally be associated with progressively diminishing visitation rates. This procedure would generate a succession of points, which could be linked to produce a curve, the precise slope of which would be given by the functional relationship arrived at above.

In the absence of an entry fee, the entire area under the demand curve would represent consumers' surplus. If no other benefits were obtained from the resource (we return to this assumption below) and if no costs arose in maintaining it, this area would also be equivalent to the total benefit from keeping the resource.

Some practical complications

The following complications may arise in using TCM:

i) **Multi-purpose visits**. Visiting site A may be part of a round-trip involving visits to other locations. It may be a detour from a journey with a different motive — *e.g.* for work, or visiting relatives. In such cases it would be incorrect to attribute the whole travel cost to the site in question. Some crude allocation of costs would be necessary, which is bound to have an arbitrary element.

ii) **Utility or extra disutility from travelling**. In many cases, travel itself is part of the pleasure of the excursion. Up to a point, a longer journey through pleasant scenery may give more pleasure than a shorter, quicker, one. Walking or cycling to a park or beach may reasonably be regarded as part of the pleasure from visiting the site. On the other hand, the objective travel cost may under-estimate the true cost of travel for people who dislike travel, or where the transport mode is unpleasant. All these considerations are likely to arise with greater force in developing countries.

iii) **Valuing leisure time**. The expenditure of leisure time on travel to a recreational or cultural amenity should not necessarily be regarded as a cost to the traveller. Up to a point, it is part of the pleasure. In principle, surveys of visitors should elicit their attitudes to travel.

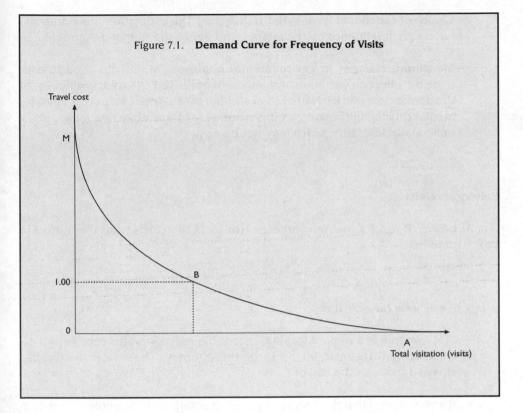

Figure 7.1. **Demand Curve for Frequency of Visits**

iv) **Sampling biases**. The costs of collecting data through questionnaire surveys tend to limit the size of sample and the period over which interviews are conducted. This could introduce a bias in favour of frequent visitors, and discourage the use of household interviews. The failure to interview non-users gives rise to **truncation bias** in the survey, and would deprive the study of important information.

v) **Non-user and off-site benefits.** TCM is a method of capturing the benefits to the direct users (*i.e.* visitors) of a site. It does not deal with off-site use values (*e.g.* watershed protection, biodiversity) or the services and goods provided to local inhabitants (wood, game, honey, medicinal products, etc.). Nor does it capture option or existence values from the resource. Hence TCM tends to underestimate total benefits. Where possible, it should be employed in conjunction with techniques that can deal with these other benefits (*e.g.* Grandstaff and Dixon, 1986).

vi) **Choice of functional form in the regression.** The estimation procedure will have a great influence on the results, and hence the demand schedule.

vii) **Measuring changes in environmental quality**. TCM may be used to estimate the effect on visitation of changes, or proposed changes, in amenity, or the demand for one site rather than another with a different level of environmental quality. In these cases it is necessary to use objective measures of environmental status, which may not be easy.

Empirical results

The kind of results that may emerge from a TCM exercise are illustrated in Box 7.1 and 7.3.

Points to note from the case study

- The example is a remote locality, accessible only by motor vehicle and attracting visitors from all parts of the country. These are favourable circumstances for the use of TCM.

- It was assumed that the sample was representative of the whole population of visitors. This would need to be tested.

- The method is not applied directly to foreign visitors, which would be a complicating feature. Instead, foreign tourists are assumed to have the same values as domestic visitors. This is probably a conservative assumption.

- The recreational value of a standing forest is only one of its potential benefits. A full catalogue would include harvestable products, ecological services, potential value of biodiversity, existence values of species, etc. Nevertheless, recreational values are among the more transparent benefits and, in principle, easy to capture in charges. It is of interest that this forest is privately owned.

- Recreational values implied by this method are convincingly in excess of those of other possible land uses, even without allowing for the other benefits of a standing forest. The policy implications for society or – in this case – the private owner are undeniable.

Box 7.3.   **Case Study: A Tropical Rain Forest in Costa Rica**

The site examined in this study is the privately owned Monteverde Cloud Forest Biological Reserve (MCFR), which straddles the continental divide in Costa Rica. The reserve consists of 10 000 ha^2 of rugged terrain, the vast majority of which is virgin rain forest. Tourism to the reserve has increased markedly over the 18 years of its existence, both in terms of domestic and foreign visitation rates, despite the relatively remote locality and difficulty of accessing the site.

The data set used in this study was collected at MCFR headquarters by the reserve management, which offered those who gave their names and addresses the opportunity to win wildlife photographs. A total of 755 of approximately 3 000 domestic visitors entered the drawing in 1988. The sample shows a similar distribution, with respect to sites of origin, as a smaller data set collected independently over 3 months during the summer of 1988. The sample was assumed to be representative of the true domestic visitor population.

Visitation rates (number of visits per 100 000 residents) were calculated for each cantón by dividing observed numbers of trips by census populations. Populations, densities, and illiteracy rates for each cantón were taken from a 1986 census. Distance is converted into currency using average cost per km estimates. We estimate that US$0.15 per km is a reasonable measure of the travel costs in Costa Rica in 1988. This estimate includes out-of-pocket costs, a fraction of fixed costs, and the value of travel time.

The linear demand functions estimated in the study suggest that visitation would drop to zero only at distances of 330-350 km. At the presumed US$15 per km, this implies a maximum price (PM) per visit of US$49-52. Domestic visitation would drop off to zero only if the price per visit exceeded US$50.

After calculating this consumer surplus for each cantón, the results are summed across all cantóns yielding an annual consumer surplus estimate of between US$97 500 and US$116 200, depending on the precise form of the demand equation. Assuming the real value of this recreational flow remains the same over time and using a real interest rate of 4 per cent, the present value of domestic recreation at this site is between US$2.4 and US$2.9 million. Given that there are about 3 000 Costa Rican visitors per year, the site is worth about US$35 per domestic visit.

This study provides the first published estimate of the ecotourism value of a tropical rain-forest reserve. The travel cost method reveals that Costa Rican citizens place a value of about US$35 per visit upon the MCFR. Tropical rain forests can generate large economic values through recreation. Domestic recreation alone represents an annual value of between US$97 500 and US$116 200 at MCFR.

This US$100 000 per year estimate does not include foreign visitors. Foreign visitors outnumbered domestic visitors by four to one in 1988. Assuming foreign tourists place the same US$35 per trip value on MCFR as domestic users do, foreign visitation would represent an additional US$400 000 to US$500 000 of international recreation value annually. In fact, foreign visitation is likely to be worth far more since foreign tourists probably value the site more than domestic visitors due to their higher income and lack of nearby substitutes.

(continued on next page)

> *(continued)*
>
> At current visitation rates, the net present value of domestic and international recreation is about US$2.5 million and US$10 million, respectively, assuming a 4 per cent real interest rate. Given that the Reserve comprises 10 000 ha^2, the combined domestic and international recreational value averages about US$1 250 per ha^2. Given that visitation has been growing at 15 per cent a year for the past five years, this present value estimate is probably far too low. Nonetheless, the price which the reserve currently pays to acquire new land is between US$30 and US$100 per ha. This suggests expansion of protected areas near this reserve is a well-justified investment, both from an economic and social perspective.
>
> *Source:* Tobias and Mendelsohn, 1991.

Overall evaluation

The TCM is a well-established method of estimating the demand for recreational facilities, and hence the benefits from their preservation and enhancement. It is no accident that the majority of empirical TCM studies have been carried out in developed countries, especially the USA. TCM works best for isolated single sites, where access is by motor vehicle, and where the characteristics of the site and its rival attractions remain constant. It is most relevant where people regard their travelling time as a cost.

The method requires a good deal of data collected from questionnaire surveys. The estimation procedure needs great care. TCM gives less clear-cut results where visits are made for several purposes. It is difficult to apply to urban sites where travel cost is small, and to visits where the travel is considered part of the benefit. The omission of local benefits, off-site and non-use values is a crucial limitation when applied, for instance, to rainforests and wildlife reserves.

TCM is a useful aid for policy decisions on: setting the level of entry fees to national parks and recreation areas; allocating national recreation and conservation budgets between different sites; judging whether it is worth preserving a site in recreational use rather than a rival land use; etc. In developing countries TCM can in addition be useful in the appraisal of fuelwood and water supply projects, where collection entails significant outlays of time and cost.

7.2. Avertive Behaviour and Defensive Expenditure

Faced with the prospect of a change in their environment, people attempt to compensate in various ways. If their environment is deteriorating, or is likely to, people will try to protect themselves against expected hardship. They will buy goods and services which help to preserve their environments. These goods may be regarded as **substitutes** or **proxies** for environmental quality. In the reverse case, where environmental quality improves, spending on these substitutes will decline.

There are various kinds of avertive behaviour (AB):

- **Defensive expenditure** (DE), sometimes called preventive spending, where people try to protect themselves against a decline in their habitat, *e.g.* by anti-soil erosion measures, installing water filters and purifiers, or putting air conditioners in their cars.

- The purchase of **environmental surrogates** is closely related to this, *e.g.* purchase of water from tankers or in bottles in preference to contaminated or unreliable public supplies.

- People who feel particularly strongly about an environmental change may opt to **relocate** themselves.

For reasons to be detailed below, AB is an imperfect measures of peoples' environmental preferences. However, it has the virtue of using the evidence of peoples' actions rather than their words, and the method is straightforward and easy to apply, compared to other valuation techniques.

This section summarises areas of application of AB, outlines the main elements in the approach, indicates some problems and qualifications applying to the method, and outlines a case study.

Areas of application

AB is potentially relevant to:

- air, water, or noise pollution;
- erosion, landslide, or flood risk;
- soil fertility, land degradation;
- marine and coastal pollution and erosion, etc.

It is appropriate where:

- people understand the environmental threats to which they are exposed;
- they take action to protect themselves;
- these actions can be costed.

AB will be most reliable for user values, where the environmental threat is directly experienced, and where action is expected to be efficacious. But the technique is unlikely to provide reliable evidence of existence values, or values for public goods.

Methods and data sources

The main steps in the use of AB methods are:

- identifying the environmental hazard;
- locating the population affected by it;
- obtaining information on their responses.

These are discussed below.

i)   Identifying the environmental hazard

This step may seem obvious, but because AB often has several motives it is important to clarify the prime environmental hazard in any situation. The growth of urban traffic will tend to increase the level of noise as well as air pollution. Problems with water supply may take the joint forms of reduced water quality and more intermittent supply. There is a fine line between building a coastal groyne to protect a beach, and building a slightly larger one to build up a beach at the expense of one's neighbour. Trees planted to protect slopes and prevent erosion have a future asset value and generate useful products.

In all these cases, taking AB values to represent environmental preferences is complicated by the existence of several behavioural motives, with multiple environmental aims. The level of DE will in such cases exaggerate values for **individual** environmental hazards. Although it may not be possible to completely isolate one environmental effect for the purpose of AB, the study should separate primary and secondary environmental issues, and ascribe AB to its principal purpose, with secondary objectives treated as bonuses.

ii)   *Locating the affected population*

For a given environmental hazard, the population at risk needs to be defined. Some cut-off point has to be drawn, delimiting populations with a vital interest in the issue, compared to those whose exposure to the hazard is so small that it can practically be disregarded. The sample for the AB study should be drawn from the first population. If excessive reliance is placed on AB evidence from populations that are only marginally affected, values will be underestimated.

The definition of the study group should normally be made pragmatically, in the light of the environmental hazard in question, and what is known about its incidence. In the case of soil erosion, for instance, effects will arise on-site and on land lower down the watershed, with further effects on downstream land and water courses. The pollution of drinking water affects people located along the water body, or within a fairly short travelling distance from it, or those using wells in the contaminated aquifer. Aircraft noise affects the population living or working in the "footprint" of airport approaches and take-off zones.

It is more difficult to define the population at risk from air pollution. The "plume" of pollution shifts, depending on seasonal and climatic conditions, as well as the level of emissions. Its incidence on the receptor population depends on the susceptibility of different individuals (*i.e.* their health), the size of maximum concentrations of pollutants, the frequency of such maxima, the presence of particularly harmful pollutants, as well as the average level. People suffering from asthma or bronchitis are especially at risk, and may take extreme measures to avoid exposure, including relocation, staying indoors during particularly bad periods of pollution, etc.

iii)   *Sources of information*

There are various ways of collecting relevant data:

- by comprehensive enquiry of all potential victims. This is feasible where relatively few parties are affected, *e.g.* a few farmers affected by erosion or downstream siltation, a hydroelectric company protecting its catchment area, industrial firms taking precautions against contamination of their water intake, sound insulation measures in major office buildings, etc.;

- sample surveys of interested parties, where there are many of them. This applies to individual householders taking precautions against declining air and water quality, or noise, farmers taking anti-erosion measures, replacing lost soil nutrients with fertilizer, etc.;

- expert opinion. Specialist opinion could be sought on the cost of defensive or precautionary measures, the cost of restoring damage or replacing environmental assets, or the purchase of environmental substitutes. This is an easy and tempting course of action. Although useful as a supplementary source of information, and as a check on the reliability of data obtained by other means, recourse to expert opinion shifts the foundations of the technique. Instead of drawing evidence from observed behaviour, this variant derives its data from views about what people **should** have done if they had been rational and well-informed.

Some complications

Although more straightforward than several other techniques, AB has its fair share of problems, the principal ones being discussed below.

i) People who are drastically affected by environmental changes will relocate. Thus studying responses among the remaining population exposed to environmental change will underestimate the real amount of DE that is occurring. Chasing up people (individuals, farmers, firms) who have relocated may be feasible, but will add to the complexity and cost of the exercise.

ii) It is virtually impossible to get perfect substitutes for environmental quality. Some goods are poor and partial substitutes for the environment, others have additional, non-environmental attributes. On the one hand, double glazing does not completely eliminate aircraft noise, but on the other hand it also improves thermal insulation and household security and requires less maintenance than other types of window. Hence spending on double glazing is a poor proxy for peace and quiet. The purchase of bottled water confers qualities (*e.g.* prestige, taste) in addition to safety and reliability. This applies to the use of RC as well, since it is rarely possible to replace environmental quality, once lost. Replacing lost soil nutrients by chemical fertilizer does not restore soil structure or minor trace elements. Planting trees to replace those removed in road building does not restore biodiversity or provide an immediate habitat for wildlife.

iii) The purchase of environmental substitutes is not a continuous decision. Most people will tolerate a certain amount of hardship or damage before they consider it worthwhile taking action. When they do act, they may judge it worthwhile to invest for the future, *e.g.* in investing in a well larger than they immediately need. In the first case, DE data lend a downward bias to estimates of the true level of damage, in the latter case they exaggerate it.

iv) The validity of DE rests on the assumption that people know the level of damage to which they are exposed, and calculate the level of DE accordingly. However, the assumption of foresight and rationality may not be warranted, especially for novel risks, or those that grow over time. People may unwittingly over- or under-compensate.

v) Even if people know how much they want to, or need to, spend, market imperfections may constrain them – *e.g.* a shortage of credit to enable farmers to undertake conservation, a physical shortage of fertilizer to replace nutrients. There is also the objection, which applies to all uses of market data in poor societies, that poverty may prevent environmental victims from spending as much to protect themselves as they would like.

Overall evaluation

Avertive behaviour techniques are relatively simple and possess a strong intuitive appeal. They use observed behaviour and draw upon data from various empirical sources, including sample surveys and expert opinion. On the other hand, data from AB methods is prone to be unreliable and difficult to interpret. In particular, AB assumes that people know the size of their environmental risk, react commensurately, and are not significantly constrained in their response, *e.g.* by poverty or market imperfections. The problem of imperfect environmental substitutes, leading to over- or under-compensation, dogs the use of AB data and invalidates much work in this area (including such popular examples as double glazing and bottled water).

In short, AB, handled with circumspection, will continue to be useful as a way of revealing the scale of peoples' environmental concerns in such areas as air and water quality, noise, land degradation, erosion and loss of fertility, the risk of landslides and flood, and coastal erosion and pollution.

It is often revealing to compare AB measures with data obtained from other techniques (especially dose-response or effects on production) in making decisions on whether to prevent environmental damage or allow it to happen, and whether to compensate victims or attempt to restore the previous environmental quality. The concept of avoided costs, commonly used as a benefit in environmental projects, is often based on empirical estimates of DE, together with Replacement Cost (Chapter 5).

7.3. Hedonic Pricing

Hedonic pricing (HP) is based on the idea that the values people place on environmental quality can be inferred from what they pay for goods incorporating environmental attributes. The market for property is usually chosen for analysis. If people consistently pay more for houses and land in one location that are identical to those elsewhere, and if every other possible non-environmental reason for the price difference is allowed for, the residual price difference is attributed to environmental factors.

HP relies on the assembly of a large amount of data on the characteristics of property in the area selected for study. Variations in its price are correlated with key features such as size, age, condition and locality, and any "unexplained" price difference is ascribed to location-specific environmental factors.

In short,

"the amenity value of cleaner air is capitalised into the value of land." (Freeman, *op cit*, p. 109).

The same kind of information can also be sought from variations in wages across different occupations and localities. All the possible reasons for wage differences are analysed – age, skill level, etc. and any residual variation is attributed to compensation for exposure to environmental or occupational risk. The theory is that labour markets will work so as to adjust wages upwards to compensate for workers' exposure to environmental risks or unpleasantness (and the reverse should also apply to work in pleasant environments). These are referred to as **wage risk** studies.

In practice, labour markets don't always work like this, especially in developing countries. Workers, especially poor and unskilled ones, are often badly informed about environmental risks, and poverty and poor environments are often cheek-by-jowl. It is common to find low wages coexisting with poor environmental conditions. Wage risk studies are of doubtful relevance, especially to developing countries, and the remainder of this section concentrates on the more common case of HP applied to property markets.

When is HP appropriate?

HP could be useful in the following cases:

- local air and water quality changes;
- noise nuisance, especially from aircraft and road traffic;

- the impact of amenity on community welfare;
- choosing the location of environmentally hazardous facilities (sewage works, power stations, etc.), planning railway or highway routes;
- evaluating the impact of neighbourhood improvement schemes in poorer parts of cities.

HP is most appropriate where:

- property markets are active;
- environmental quality is perceived by the population as a relevant factor in property values;
- local variations in environmental quality, or changes over time, are clearly perceptible;
- property markets are relatively undistorted and transactions are transparent.

The main steps in HP

The following are the principal stages in HP:

- defining and measuring the environmental attribute;
- specifying the hedonic price function;
- collecting cross-sectional or time series data;
- using multiple regression analysis to value the environmental attribute;
- deriving the demand curve for environmental improvement.

These are described below.

i)   *Measuring the environmental attribute*

Environmental status must be susceptible to measurement if it is to be correlated with property prices. Air quality, for instance, can be represented by various indicators – the concentration of various gases (CO_2, NO_x, SO_2, ozone, etc.) and by the presence of particulates. The analogous indicators for water quality are dissolved oxygen content, biological oxygen demand, coliform count, etc.

The choice of indicators will depend on the purpose in hand. If the effect of air and water quality on health is of particular concern, the most relevant indicators will be those known to be strongly correlated with health, *e.g.* sulphate particulates (for air pollution) and coliform count (for swimming water). Some environmental attributes are difficult to measure, *e.g.* air visibility (important for amenity and aesthetic benefits) or clarity of water (for diving and snorkelling).

Noise levels are normally expressed in decibels, but for different purposes or individuals the average ambient level, the maximum noise level, or the frequency of high decibel levels could each be most relevant. People regularly exposed to noise may become inured (although objectively affected) to relatively high levels of ambient noise, but sensitive to extreme levels. Certain kinds of noise are more troublesome than others.

Having chosen the appropriate environmental indicator, the next decision concerns its **critical range**. Changes in, say, air and water quality may make little difference to property values at low levels of pollution. But the same proportionate changes may be significant once the absolute level approaches and exceeds some critical point (**threshold level**). For other environmental indicators, the relationship between the build up of pollution and its effect on the receptor may be linear, which is easier to model in HP.

ii) Specifying the hedonic price function

This stage consists of specifying the functional relationship between the price of property and all its relevant characteristics, including its environmental attributes. The explanatory variables are likely to include:

- property characteristics (number of rooms, age, size of plot, possession of garage, condition, etc.);

- location and neighbourhood factors (access to transport services, local facilities, shopping, proximity to busy road and rail routes, crime rate, perceptions of neighbourhood "quality", etc.);

- environmental attributes (measures of air and water quality, noise, amenity, etc.) in each of the different areas;

For certain purposes, a fourth group of indicators will be necessary, namely:

- socioeconomic characteristics of individual property owners (age, income, family status, educational qualifications, profession, etc.).

The choice of variables will obviously influence the results of the study. If too few variables are chosen, the unexplained residual will be exaggerated, thereby overestimating the value of the environmental attribute. But if too many variables are chosen, apart from overburdening data collection, this could produce **correlation bias**.

The choice of functional form is an important technical issue which will affect benefit estimates. A common choice is the semi-log form, though a number of others are available. Statistical advice should be sought on the precise functional form (OECD, 1994).

iii)   Data collection

HP requires the assembly of large amounts of data. Property prices should ideally be drawn from an active market representative of the different kinds of property and the different zones to be sampled. The evidence should be expressed in constant prices and net of property tax. In practice data is usually obtained from the records of estate (property) agents or, more informally, from canvassing their expert opinions.

Cross-sectional or time series data can be used. The former, which compares different property transactions within the same time period, is usually preferred where the data set is large enough to form an adequate sample. The use of time series data, comparing changes in the same type of property over different time periods, may be invalid if strong trend factors have been present, or if there have been changes in taste or other structural parameters. However, in straightforward "before and after" comparisons, *e.g.* in neighbourhood improvement schemes in poor communities, time series analysis may be valid.

The case study discussed below used a large computerised data set kept by a leading national firm of estate agents in a country with an active and transparent property market. Not all studies take place in such propitious circumstances. Where markets are inactive, controlled, distorted or segmented, or where transactions occur informally or deviously, the collection of reliable price data is problematic.

iv)   Correlation

In this stage, multiple regression analysis is used to obtain a correlation between property values and the chosen environmental attribute. Price is regressed on all the non-environmental variables separately, and price differentials are "explained" in these terms. Any remaining unexplained price differential is then correlated with the chosen environmental attribute, *e.g.* air quality, proximity to good scenery. This attribute may be expressed as an index (*e.g.* for air quality, the % presence of potentially undesirable chemical elements), or as a dummy variable (absence or presence of the attribute, signified respectively by 0 or 1).

The result of this correlation is to produce the **implicit price** of the attribute, say air quality. In the prevailing market, an individual wishing to obtain better air quality, for a given type of property, tends to have to pay this implicit price.

v)   Deriving a demand curve for environmental improvement

In theory, a further step is necessary to derive the individual's willingness to pay (WTP) for the environment. This environmental WTP (or **bid function**) may differ from the estimation produced by the market, in much the same way that an individual's WTP for a house may differ from the price dictated by the market (or its estate agent acolytes).

The implicit price of the environmental attribute obtained by regression analysis is likely to reflect WTP if the measured level of the attribute corresponds to that perceived by the household concerned. In short, subjective and objective environmental perceptions may or may not coincide.

To obtain a more accurate estimate of WTP the implicit price of the environmental attribute should be regressed against individuals' socioeconomic characteristics. This further stage entails advanced estimation techniques, and specialist statistical advice should be sought at this point.

Qualifications to the use of HP

HP is a sophisticated and complex technique with a huge appetite for data. The problems it gives rise to can be summarized as follows:

i)   property markets may not be sufficiently active, transparent and smoothly-functioning to generate reliable data;

ii) even where they are, a large amount of data has to be collected and processed, with considerable demands for statistical and econometric skills;

iii) the environmental variable may not be measurable;

iv) individuals in the property market perceive environmental problems in a subjective way. The leap from estimating implicit prices to deriving WTP is a difficult one;

v) results depend heavily on the functional form and estimation techniques; because the environmental factor is equated with the residual in a regression, the specification of the function is critical;

vi) property prices may embody the market's anticipation of future trends and events, including likely environmental changes.

Overall evaluation

HP should not be undertaken lightly. It has a formidable need for data and requires statistical and econometric skills of a high order. Its precondition is a well-functioning and transparent property market in which environmental attributes are clearly perceived and valued by individual property owners. The results are sensitive to the choice of functional forms and estimating procedures.

These factors seriously limit its applicability. In practice it has been used on large-scale studies of the impact of air pollution, aircraft noise and amenity on property values. It does not capture non-use values, hence underestimates total environmental values. Cruder versions of HP can be used to estimate the benefits of neighbourhood improvement schemes in poorer cities (Box 7.4).

Box 7.4. **Visakhapatnam Slum Improvement Programme (SIP)**

Visakhapatnam lies on the east coast of India, midway between Calcutta and Madras. Between 1971 and 1991, its population trebled from 360 000 to 1.05 million. This rapid increase reflected the city's industrial growth as a major naval base and manufacturing centre, the poverty of the surrounding rural areas from which many migrate, and the high natural birth rate. However, there is an acute shortage of land in the city which is bounded by hills and sea. Population density is high, with 30 000 persons per km^2 over much of the city. Despite some industrial prosperity, over 200 000 people (40 000 households) live in nearly 200 officially designated slums with an average annual household income of 13 000 rupees ($400). Half the adults in the slums are illiterate. Few slum households have private tap water and only half of the slums have public tap water. Under one in five slum houses has a toilet and 60 per cent of slum dwellers practise open defecation. Not surprisingly, health problems are rife.

In 1988 the Visakhapatnam Municipal Corporation, supported by the UK Overseas Development Administration, started a major programme to improve 170 slums. This programme included physical infrastructure improvements (roads, drainage, paths, street lighting), improved water supply, public toilets, community centres, primary health care services, and educational and training services. Concurrently, the Municipal Corporation provided subsidised housing loans to slum residents to improve their dwellings.

When slum improvements are formally evaluated, benefits are almost always based on estimated increases in land values or rents. For example, World Bank studies forecast that increased land values or rents would produce real rates of return of between 15 and 19 per cent for slum improvement programmes in Madhya Pradesh, Uttar Pradesh and Calcutta and estimated an ex-post 23 per cent rate of return for slum improvements in Madras.

Under certain conditions, nearly all private benefits (including health, productivity and amenity benefits) would be reflected in increased land prices or rents, and in house prices, in the slums. These conditions are:

i) all private benefits accrue only to residents of the slum area;
ii) all SIP benefits (including health benefits, reduced flood and fire damages etc.) are fully perceived by people inside and outside the slum areas;
iii) slum property prices are not controlled; slum residents can sell or rent their properties to outsiders as well as to other slum residents; and
iv) property transactions are costless.

Even under these conditions, there would usually be some residual householder (consumer) surpluses. For example, it is unlikely that the full benefits of the training programmes or health care would be precisely capitalised in property values.

Visakhapatnam has an active housing market. Official (Land Registration Department) records indicate that 1.5 to 2.0 per cent of the housing stock is sold each year. Recorded sales in the slums are lower due to restrictions on sales. But there are many unofficial ("benami") sales where prices are known locally. Of course, houses sold under restrictions sell at a discount. Also, there are fewer land than house sales. Therefore land values must be Inferred from house prices or based on valuation data. The benefits of the city-wide SIP were estimated from increases in land values, house prices and rents.

(continued on next page)

(continued)

Official land valuation data were collected for typical properties in 24 slum areas which were improved in 1988 or 1989 and valued (to the nearest R 50 per square yard) in 1987 and 1990. Between these two years, mean land values in the sample slums increased from R 256 to R 441 per square yard. Elsewhere in Visakhapatnam land values rose by an estimated average 20 per cent except in commercial development areas where land values rose by another 10 to 20 per cent. Allowing for an overall increase in land values in Visakhapatnam of 25 per cent, average slum land values would have risen to R 320 without the SIP and the difference between R 441 and R 320 is attributable to the SIP. Applying a benefit of R 121 per square yard to 36 500 houses with an average 50 square yards per house (a total of 1 825 million square yards) produces a total increase in land values of R 221 million in 1990 Rs or about R 254 million in 1992 Rs.

The estimated benefits from the land value and house price approaches are reassuringly close and give one some confidence in the results.

Alternatively, in competitive markets, increased rents could be a measure of improved living conditions. Between 1988 and 1991, the average rent of Visakhapatnam slum tenants who pay rent increased from R 114/month to R 145/month in 1992 prices. Applying a notional annual rent increase of R 372 to 36 500 slum households, total rent increases would be R 13.6 million per annum. With a 10 per cent discount rate, the capital equivalent would be R 136 million.

This figure is well below the estimated increase in land values or house prices and cannot be considered relevant to evaluation of the SIP. The relatively low rate of return can be explained partly by the unrepresentative nature of the rental market: only 13 per cent of households are tenants and they mostly rent in the lower to middle end of the slum housing market. Also, restrictions on tenant evictions substantially reduce market rents.

In conclusion, the Visakhapatnam Municipal Corporation has spent about R 300 million on improving 170 slums. An additional R 20 million or more per annum will probably be required to maintain this capital programme. The SIP brings benefits to slum and non-slum households, and savings to the government.

In short, most slum household benefits are reflected in increased land and house prices, although some benefits may not be fully capitalised into property prices. We estimated that the SIP increased total land values in the 170 slums by R 254 million and house prices by R 285 million. Allowing for some slum householder surpluses, private non-slum benefits and government savings (equivalent in total to about one-quarter of SIP costs), there is a clear surplus of social benefit over capital expenditures.

Source: Abelson, 1995.

Further References and Sources

General expositions of the travel cost method, the hedonic property technique and the defensive expenditure approach are contained in several of the texts cited at the end of Chapter 3, *e.g.* OECD (1994), Freeman (1993), Hufschmidt *et al.* (1983). The quotation from Freeman in Section 7.3 is from the previous (1979) edition of this book.

Specific references used in this chapter are as follows:

WALSH, Richard G., JOHNSON, Donn M. and McKEAN, John R., "Benefit transfer of outdoor recreation demand studies, 1968-88", *Water Resources Research*, 28/3, 1992.

TOBIAS, Dave and MENDELSOHN, Robert, "Valuing ecotourism in a tropical rain-forest reserve", *Ambio*, Vol. 20, No. 2, April 1991.

ABELSON, Peter, *Project appraisal and valuation methods for the environment, with special reference to developing countries*, to be published by Macmillan, London, 1995.

Chapter 8

DEALING WITH TIME

Costs and benefits arising in the future have a lower value than those arising now. The more distant in time they occur, the less they are valued. Discounting is the process of adjusting future sums to arrive at their present value.

Discounting has become an integral part of conventional cost-benefit analysis (CBA). CBA is an objective method of assessing and comparing projects according to their respective net benefits. Projects with the same net benefits over a 20-year period will not be of equal attractiveness if one has its net benefits bunched in the first ten years, and the other in the later ten years of the period. Discounting, which is the inverse of compound interest, reduces future values of costs and benefits dramatically (Box 8.1)

There are two main reasons why discounting is used:

- **Time preference.** Individuals prefer to enjoy benefits sooner, and costs later, rather than the other way round. A cost or benefit of a given amount has a lower subjective value, the later it arises. This may be due to myopia, an urgent need for gratification (*e.g.* because of poverty or greed), or the belief that future consumption will be greater (and therefore the marginal utility of a given unit of consumption will be less). These factors apply to private individuals. Governments, acting in a rational and enlightened way on behalf of their citizens, may also have **social** time preference, for example where they expect future incomes to be greater, and where $1 now is worth more to society than the same in future.

- **Opportunity cost of capital**. A sum of money is worth more now than the same amount in future because it can be employed productively, *e.g.* invested profitably, or lent for interest. In this case the discount rate is the inverse of the rate of interest. Funds used on a project which generates a given return on some future date could have been used to generate returns immediately. A discount rate reminds us of this alternative use of funds. Discounting assists the rational allocation of capital between uses that have different temporal profiles.

Box 8.1. **The power of discounting**

The discount factor (DF) of a future amount at the end of the nth period at an interest rate of i is given by the formula:

$$DF = 1/(1 + i)^n.$$

Thus, applied to a sum of $100 arising in year 8, at an interest rate of 10 per cent, the discount factor is 0.466 and the discounted value (= present value) of the sum is $46.6. Many computer programmes and the more powerful calculators have the capability of calculating present values. Published tables of discount rates may also be consulted for manual calculations.

At a rate of compound interest of 10 per cent, a sum of $1 grows to over $10.8 at the end of 25 years. Conversely, at a discount rate of 10 per cent, the offer of $1 in 25 years time is only equivalent to $0.09 (nine cents) today.

At this discount rate, a given benefit or cost stream loses half its value after 7 years. At 10 per cent, extending the analysis for longer than 15 years is of little value since the future stream is so heavily discounted.

Using a lower discount rate, however, would make a substantial difference. At 5 per cent, a net benefit stream would lose half its value after year 14, and in year 25 would still be worth almost 30 per cent of its initial amount.

There is a sizeable literature on the theoretical aspects of discounting (OECD, 1994). Its use as a practical tool in the choice of investments has also attracted much discussion, and some controversy. One reason is that a single discount rate is expected to perform several different, and often incompatible, purposes. For instance, it is only if certain restrictive theoretical conditions are satisfied that the rate of time preference would coincide with the opportunity cost of capital.

The difficulties are compounded in the appraisal of environmental projects, when other, incompatible, objectives are heaped onto the discount rate.

This chapter has three main sections. The first addresses some of the problems of estimating appropriate discount rates. The second rehearses some of the implications of the choice of discount rate for projects with environmental effects. The third proposes some practical ways of tackling appraisal, retaining discounting while recognising concerns for the environment and the interests of future generations.

8.1. Estimating the Social Rate of Discount

In many situations analysts are given a specific rate of discount to work with. The same is true of officials: many governments and agencies adopt a particular discount rate to apply to all public investment projects, and the estimation of the "correct" rate does not arise.

However, both analysts and officials sometimes need to estimate or adjust discount rates used in project appraisal. In any case, it is important to understand the *raison d'être* of the discount rate used in appraisal and ensure that the chosen rate is defensible on **economic** grounds, before any environmental concerns are considered. A common environmental critique is that discount rates are typically set too high even in economic terms.

There is a different discount rate corresponding to each of the various concepts – the social rate of time preference, the accounting rate of interest, the consumer discount rate, the producer discount rate, or some synthetic rate based on the above (OECD, 1994). There have been some attempts to derive empirical values for the above concepts.

Social opportunity cost of capital

One possible short-cut estimation method is to take the real long term rate of return on equity capital as a proxy for the opportunity cost of capital. This would be appropriate where an investment would displace a project of a similar size in the private sector. In countries with well developed financial markets, this information is normally readily available from financial analysts. This measure does, however, include an average premium for risk, which would not be appropriate for riskless **public** investments. Another problem is that many newly-emerging financial markets have a narrow trading base and are distorted in various ways.

In other situations, the long term lending and borrowing rates in low risk or risk-free markets (*e.g.* rates on long term bonds issued by a reputable government) may be used.

Social time preference

Society should, in theory, favour present over future consumption for two main reasons. Firstly, because of pure time preference, as for individuals. secondly, because of expected growth in incomes, and the related point that the increments in those incomes are subject to diminishing marginal value (marginal utility). Although the concept can readily be grasped at an intuitive level, calculating the social rate of time preference (or consumption rate of interest) is difficult (Box 8.2).

Box 8.2.   **Estimating Social Time Preference**

The social time preference is defined by the formula:

$$s = p + u.g$$

where
s = social rate of time preference
p = pure rate of time preference, the rate at which utility is discounted
u = rate at which marginal utility declines as consumption increases
g = expected growth in consumption per head

Source: (OECD, 1994).

Calculations of p are more or less arbitrary: several studies have produced estimates of up to 2 per cent, though these have been done for developed countries. g can be calculated from projections of incomes and population. u is an elusive concept: figures of 1-2 per cent have been produced by some studies, though they have been challenged.

Synthetic discount rates

Since theoretical principles give ambiguous guidance on the best discount rate to choose for practical purposes, the use of a synthetic rate is attractive. One version derives a social discount rate, w, from a weighted average of the rate of social time preference and the opportunity cost of capital. The weights are the proportions of benefits that are respectively consumed and invested. The formula is given in Box 8.3.

The attempt to justify the selection of a discount rate applying to public investment projects in the UK is illustrated in Box 8.4.

Comments on case study

i) The level chosen for the RRR was arrived at as a compromise between considerations of social time preference and the opportunity cost of capital.

ii) Values for p and u, crucial to the estimation of social time preference, have no direct empirical basis.

Box 8.3.   **Use of Synthetic Discount Rates**

The synthetic discount rate, w, is defined by:

$$w = h1.r + h2.s$$

where
- h1 = the share of investment in national income, as a proxy for the fraction of government spending displacing private investment;
- h2 = the share of consumption in national income, as a proxy for the fraction of government spending displacing private consumption;
- s = rate of social time preference;
- r = average real rate of return on private capital, as a proxy for the marginal opportunity cost of capital.

Thus, if h1 and h2 are respectively 20 per cent and 80 per cent, s is 2 per cent and r is 8 per cent (all these values are realistic), w will be 3.2 per cent.

---

iii) The RRR is lower than that used in the past, and lower than those applied by most aid agencies. This partly reflects the average yield on capital in a mature developed economy and an assumed low level of time preference and elasticity of the marginal utility of income in this relatively affluent society. The value for the RRR should not necessarily be taken as a guide for discount rates in rapidly growing or poorer countries (Box 8.5).

8.2. Discounting and the Environment

Certain features of discounting have been highlighted as potentially damaging to environmental concerns. These are:

- Damage to the environment likely to arise in the long term is reduced to insignificance by discounting. The costs of a future natural catastrophe, or of future loss of habitat, or groundwater contamination might not register in the scales of a CBA compared to more immediate costs. It is argued that many environmental risks are only likely to appear in the long term.

- Conversely, projects yielding environmental benefits in the more distant future would not receive a fair hearing compared to those with short term benefits, since their benefits would be heavily discounted. It is argued that discounting discriminates against "environmental" projects.

Box 8.4. **Case Study: The Required Rate of Return (RRR)**
on UK Public Investment

The RRR is currently set at 6 per cent by the British Treasury. This means that proposed UK public investments should be expected to earn a real rate of return of at least 6 per cent. This is the discount rate to which proposed uses of public funds should be subjected. This note summarises an exercise to justify the choice of this particular rate.

It is accepted that considerations of social time preference and the opportunity cost of capital may conflict in setting the appropriate discount rate. The figure of 6 per cent is taken as a rate that would serve both purposes, though this is not an average based on any formal weighting system.

In setting an **opportunity cost of capital**, the options are to take the government borrowing rate or the private sector costs of capital. The government borrowing rate gives a lower value than the private sector costs, because it excludes tax, and is practically risk-free. The respective long term levels of these two rates was, in 1990, taken to be 4 per cent and 6 per cent.

It was considered to be difficult to infer **time preference** from market rates. The government borrowing rate, though risk-free, is rejected as a guide, because of the various other factors (such as liquidity preference) which affect the interest rates at which people lend and borrow). Each of the two theoretical determinants of time preference is considered.

Pure time preference [p in our notation above] is taken to be 1.5 per cent ("... a matter partly of judgement...not implausible or inconsistent with the literature..." p. 82). Likewise, the elasticity of the marginal utility of consumption [u in our notation] is also taken to be 1.5 per cent for similar reasons. It is then pointed out that, with an expected growth rate of national income per head of 2.5 per cent, these values of p and u imply a rate of time preference in the range 4-6 per cent.

Source: H.M. Treasury, 1991, Appendix to Annex G.

- The use of high discount rates hastens the rate of exploitation of renewable natural resources, such as forests, fisheries and game. This lends an "exploitative" rather than a "conservationist" bias to the exploitation of concessions. In extreme cases, where the discount rate exceeds the rate of natural regeneration, it is rational to harvest a resource to extinction.

- For these reasons, the interests of future generations are not properly safeguarded. Investment decisions are myopic and "anti-future".

Adherents of these views propose various solutions:

- low or zero discount rates;
- the application of lower discount rates to environmental projects or specific environmental effects;

Box 8.5.   **Estimating Discount Rates in Developing Countries**

The choice of discount rates is a rough and ready process, even in countries with well-developed capital markets. Several key elements in the calculation are the fruits of guess and assumption. International agencies commonly apply discount rates in the range 8-12 per cent in real terms on behalf of their recipients, but these levels have been challenged as being too high, particularly in developing countries (Cline, 1993).

Using the concepts in Boxes 8.2 and 8.3, the considerations involved in setting a country-specific discount rate are the following:

- growth in consumption per head, a product of expected growth in incomes and population. In the past decade this has ranged from below zero in stagnant poor countries, through 15 per cent for middle/upper middle developing countries, to about 4 per cent for China and India combined;
- the decline in marginal utility as consumption increases. This is an arbitrary figure, commonly taken to be between 1 and 2;
- the rate of "pure" time preference, also arbitrary, often taken to be between 1 and 2.

The above items, when combined according to the formula in Box 8.2, produce a rate of social time preference (= consumption rate of interest) of minus 0.4 to minus 0.8 per cent for low income countries, 0.4 to 0.8 per cent for lower middle income countries, 1.4-2.8 for upper middle income countries, 2.5-5.0 per cent for high income countries, and 4-8 per cent for India and China combined (OECD, 1994, p. 206). This figure should then be combined with:

- The opportunity cost of capital, sometimes estimated from the average real rate of return on private capital. In rapidly growing economies this can be very high, and in most cases is unlikely to fall below 8 per cent.

Using the weights as in Box 8.3:

- The respective shares of consumption and investment in national income, which could be taken as 80 per cent and 20 per cent respectively.

Using the values for the above variables as indicated, and combining them in the formulae of Boxes 8.2 and 8.3 would produce national discount rates in the region of 3-4 per cent. This is significantly lower than those that tend to be used, and there may be good reasons why governments choose levels of test discount rates different from those that would be indicated by the above theoretical considerations.

- applying distributional weights to costs and benefits accruing to future generations.

Some of these are impractical. For instance, they require a clear distinction to be tenable between "environmental" and other projects, or between "environmental" and other effects within the same projects. Using distributional weights to benefit future generations is fraught with philosophical, moral, economic and practical problems. It is a highly subjective and arbitrary process which, for good reasons, has made little headway in conventional CBA. Introducing differential discount rates could also distort capital markets where government and private investors are active in the same sectors.

They are also undesirable. It is a bad idea, as a matter of principle, to apply low discount rates in poor countries that are short of capital. This would:

- Encourage the use of capital-intensive schemes. This would discourage employment, and thus increase poverty, which often increases pressures on the environment. It would also promote schemes with dubious environmental credentials, such as hydroelectric schemes, as compared to relatively clean thermal options such as gas-fired fluidised bed combustion (because the former would have a higher initial cost and higher long term net benefits compared to the latter).

- Allow more unproductive schemes to proceed, namely those unable to meet the normal required rate of return. This would increase the use of natural resources and encroachment on hitherto undeveloped areas. More generally, it would result in the wasteful use of capital.

In the first section above it was argued that the discount rate is often asked to do too much. As a device for allocating capital between projects and over time discounting is irreplaceable, even though there is room for debate about the appropriate rate to use. It is better to try to deal with particular environmental concerns directly, and leave discounting to fulfil its basic purpose. We turn to some practical steps in the final section.

8.3. Living with Discounting

The recommended approach is to use whatever the normal discount rate is for all projects, and to attempt to deal with particular environmental concerns directly, rather than by adjusting the discount rate. Some of the environmental concerns surrounding the use of discounting in CBA can be met without abandoning this useful device – which would be an unnecessary sacrifice giving rise to distortions of its own.

Concerns about **future environmental risks** may be quite legitimate. There are acceptable methods of dealing with risk and uncertainty which are discussed in Chapter 10. A serious future risk which has a low probability will, indeed, be heavily discounted, but if decision-makers are risk-averse a project can be modified to suit them. Future environmental damage is often undervalued because too little is known about the processes involved. In such cases, action lies in the realm of investment in information and risk management (Chapter 9), rather than discounting *per se*.

Justice to future generations is controversial, and difficult to translate into operational principles. It is especially tricky where future generations are expected to be materially better off, and have substantially different lifestyles. If the principle means keeping options open, it implies preserving biodiversity, keeping variety in representative landscapes and habitats, avoiding the extinction of species, slowing down the exploitation of scarce finite resources, collecting data and investing in information about the natural world and environmental processes. Discounting is peripheral to many of these worthy aims, and its abandonment could have the perverse effects noted earlier.

Many environmental concerns can be addressed by more complete **economic valuation.** From the environmental point of view, for any given discount rate, too many damaging projects, and too few beneficent ones, are approved because the costs and benefits in question are not identified and valued. The growing practice of environmental economic valuation is calling attention to these hidden items, and leading to a shift in portfolio choice in directions of which environmentalists would approve.

Many economists now accept the need for a balanced approach to environmental CBA, including discounting, full environmental valuation, and application of the **sustainability criterion** introduced in Chapter 1 and Box 1.4. This criterion has different implications depending on whether the resources in question are critical, renewable, or finite.

Using irreplaceable **critical natural capital** should be avoided, so far as possible. This is a matter of project design and the search for alternatives. Economists may reasonably point out that certain environmental assets are becoming scarcer and society's appreciation of them is increasing. In some situations the cost of alternatives (*e.g.* thermal power production rather than damming an attractive valley) could fall over time and thus the opportunity cost of avoiding their use will diminish. Using an increasing implicit factor to value a benefit stream, and a diminishing factor on the (opportunity) cost side amounts to using a falling discount rate. In plain terms, an increasing implicit environment benefit is being obtained for a reducing opportunity cost.

The use of **renewable natural capital** should be fully debited to a project. If a project uses a natural resource within its sustainable yield (*e.g.* a forest, fishery or aquifer) the cost to the project is the economic "rent" from its extraction, normally estimated as the residual when all other production costs have been subtracted from its price. If the use of the resource exceeds its sustainable yield, a cost should be debited to the project equal to that of regenerating the resource (*e.g.* replanting, restocking) or of the potential damage incurred (*e.g.* an aquifer contaminated through overuse).

The process of debiting a project with its environmental costs could be either notional or actual. There is increasing interest in making compensation actual, entailing real payments of some kind. Where damage or overexploitation is caused by a number of separate projects, where feasible a compensatory project should be undertaken which restores the environment. The cost of this project would be attributed to each of the projects responsible for the damage.

In the case of finite **non-renewable resources**, sustainability means setting aside part of sales proceeds for investment to maintain consumption after the resource is exhausted. It also means investing in research into alternatives, and into more efficient ways of using it so that future generations are not cheated of discoveries relying on the continuing supply of the resource.

Conclusion

Discounting has inspired an extensive economic literature, to which has recently been added the critical attention of environmentalists. The theoretical arguments about the case for discounting, the choice of different variants, and the problems of estimation, are by no means resolved. The best guidance to give to practitioners is still rough and ready.

The discount rate performs several functions, notably to signal time preference and to allocate capital according to its opportunity cost. Estimating social time preference is difficult and in practice most attempts fall back on hunch and assumption. Deriving empirical proxies for the opportunity cost of capital is possible, but there are several sources giving different values. Synthetic discount rates combine the two in a weighted average. The result is usually that the two approaches give different values within a range.

Discounting does not satisfactorily deal with all aspects of the appraisal of projects with significant environmental implications. However, dropping discounting, or tampering with the rate, is impractical, undesirable, or both. The canon of environmental appraisal needs to evolve in a pragmatic way. Many difficult issues arise and need to be resolved by experienced and well-intentioned practitioners.

It is recommended that:

- environmental appraisal includes the use of conventional discount rates;
- the actual discount rate used should be critically examined following principles set out in this chapter;
- environmental costs and benefits should be properly valued;
- any long term change in the expected relative value of environmental assets should be reflected in their appraisal prices;
- the sustainability criterion should be used, implying the avoidance of critical natural capital and entering the cost of resources that are used in excess of their sustainable yield.

Further References and Sources

There is a thorough review of the discounting issue, with a proposed *modus operandi*, and discussion of the "sustainability constraint" in the following:

MARKANDYA, A. and PEARCE, D., *Environmental considerations and the choice of the discount rate in developing countries*. World Bank Environment Department Working Paper No. 9, Washington, DC, 1988.

There is an interesting debate on environmental discounting in the following two articles:

BIRDSALL, Nancy and STEER, Andrew, "Act now on global warming – but don't cook the books"; and

CLINE, William, "Give greenhouse abatement a fair chance".

Both articles are in *Finance and Development*, Vol. 30, No. 1, 1993. Washington, DC.

Other references in the chapter are as follows:

HM TREASURY, *Economic appraisal in Central Government: A Technical Guide for Government Departments*, HMSO, London, 1991.

Chapter 9

RISK AND UNCERTAINTY

The outcome of most human activities cannot be accurately predicted. This may be due to **ignorance** of the possible outcomes, which is an extreme case of **uncertainty** about future events. As our knowledge improves, we may be able to express our uncertainty about future outcomes in terms of the **probability** of them happening. In this case, we have converted uncertainty into **risk**. Risk has been described as measurable uncertainty.

Although all human interventions in nature are prone to some uncertainty, this is the very essence of projects with major environmental effects. Many environmental processes are still very poorly understood, hence we cannot be confident about their environmental impact. We may understand the type of impact that is likely, but not its scale, or timing. It is especially difficult to anticipate the eventual impact of something which sets off a chain reaction, or triggers complex feed-back processes, or which has a cumulative effect. **Irreversible** effects, such as extinction of a species, damage to the ozone layer or permanent modification of a landscape, are of particular concern.

Faced with uncertainty, the economist can contribute in various ways:

i) make the case for investment in information;
ii) present the various possible outcomes, with their probabilities (risk assessment);
iii) take into account the perceptions and preferences of the decision-maker and/or the general public (risk perception and subjective preferences);
iv) devise appropriate decision rules and investment strategies (risk management).

The chapter is organised on the above lines. A case study is described, drawn from a Caribbean country, dealing with various risks posed by untreated sewage.

9.1. Investing in Information

Where environmental effects are uncertain, but believed to be potentially large, it makes obvious sense to produce more information about them. Commissioning an Environmental Impact Assessment (EIA) is one way of doing this, and EIAs are mandatory for many types of investments in a number of countries. Setting up pilot schemes, in which environmental effects can be tested in controlled circumstances, is another method. Funding scientific research is another possibility.

In many cases, information will already exist, and the role of the economist would be to marshall data in a way that is germane to the decision in question. It might, for example, be illuminating to compare the costs of alternative methods of meeting water or air quality standards using the cost-effectiveness criterion. It is also important to estimate the **opportunity costs** incurred where a project is delayed or abandoned. There may also be the eventual extra cost of modifying the project to take into account the new information.

There is also a value attached to avoiding irreversible actions. This is an **option value**. Any information which increases our knowledge about future environmental effects has so-called **quasi-option value**. These are the benefits from investing in information. Any delay in starting a project has an option value, in that it keeps open a choice which would be foreclosed if the project went ahead immediately. This option value could be very large for projects with irreversible environmental effects. Identifying an environmental problem earlier, rather than after the project is implemented, may avoid more expensive modifications later. Moreover, more accurate knowledge about an effect could reduce the size of the safety margin built into a project following the Precautionary Principle (Box 9.1).

Economic analysis is severely constrained by the presence of uncertainty. However, one useful exercise is to perform **sensitivity analysis** on the main variables in a project or policy analysis. Suppose a particular environmental change may happen, but cannot be assigned a probability. Suppose further that this would affect the costs and benefits of the project. Although the probability of the effect cannot be specified, the sensitivity of the project (or policy) to this change can be illustrated by showing how the rate of return or NPV would respond to a given change in each environmentally-sensitive variable. Because a central (most likely) value for the variables cannot be given, upper and lower bound estimates are produced.

The same information can be presented in a different way using **switching values**. These show the critical values for each variable in the analysis, namely the size of change that would reduce the NPV to zero, or the rate of return to the cut-off level. High values can be disregarded, because they imply that very large changes would be necessary to

---

Box 9.1. **The Precautionary Principle and Other Rules**

The Precautionary Principle may come into its own where the parties are very risk averse, or where decisions have to be taken in the face of uncertainty over potentially important environmental impacts. In its extreme form, it holds that no actions should be taken if there is the remotest risk of substantial environmental damage. In its more practical guise, the principle states that the risk of substantial environmental damage should be avoided, provided that the cost of doing so, including the opportunity cost of inaction, is "reasonable". What is "reasonable" can only be decided by the parties themselves.

A related concept is that of the **Safe Minimum Standard** (SMS). The SMS applies a modified version of the minimax criterion (see a later part of this chapter), preferring the option which minimises the maximum possible loss that could result from making the wrong decision. This alternative should be chosen unless the costs of doing so are unacceptably large. What is "unacceptably large" is, once again, left to the decision maker to decide, depending on the context.

The **critical load** of a substance is the maximum annual amount that an area, habitat or receptor body can safely absorb and tolerate. It may apply to the capacity of the atmosphere to assimilate pollutants, or a river or lake to absorb untreated sewage or industrial effluent. Once the critical load is exceeded, the function of natural assimilation is impaired or destroyed. In certain cases, this may be irreversible.

---

substantially affect the NPV of the whole project. On the other hand, small values are worth noting, because they mean that relatively small movements in a certain variable can make or break the entire project. This information enables the decision-maker to focus on factors which are vital to the performance of the project (Box 9.2).

9.2. Risk Assessment

Risk assessment is the process of converting uncertainty into risk. It entails three main steps:

- analysing the initiating events and the routes (pathways) through which the effect occurs;
- specifying the size and severity of the risk;
- estimating probabilities and expected values.

i)   *Identifying the pathways*

The first of the above steps entails analysing the process and breaking it down into manageable parts for the purpose of assigning probabilities. In the case of an

Box 9.2. **Switching Values in Djibouti Forestry Project (Ahmad, 1993)**

Benefit stream	Appraisal present value	Switching present value	Per cent change
Forage production	607 832	312 375	−48
Wood production	25 704	−269 783	−1.149
Charcoal production	80 907	−214 580	−365
Avoidance of loss	75 932	−219 555	−389
Apiculture	17 054	−278 433	−1.732
Aviculture	2 396	−293 091	−12.330
Woodcraft	24 008	−271 497	−1.230
Total benefits	**833 866**	**538 378**	**−35**
Total cost	**538 378**	**833 866**	**54**

The above Table shows switching values (SVs) for a forestry and land rehabilitation project in Djibouti. The first column indicates the present value (discounted future stream) of seven different kinds of benefit expected from the project (forage production, wood, etc.). The second column contains the equivalent SV for each benefit, which is the amount by which it would need to fall in order to reduce the NPV of the whole project to zero, if all other costs and benefits stay constant. The final column expresses the SV as a % of the original amount.

The decision-maker has to look out for SVs that are relatively low, since this would signify that small changes in particular items would be enough to wreck the project. In this case, the lowest SV is for forage production: if this benefit fell to approximately half its expected value, the project would have a zero NPV. All the other benefits have roughly similar SVs, and are all negative. This indicates that the benefits expected from charcoal, wood, beekeeping, etc. would not only have to disappear, but would have to become huge (and totally implausible) negative amounts for the project to founder.

The conclusion to be drawn from this example is that the project is reasonably robust, and only a halving in the size of its major benefit would cause it to become unviable.

industrial process or power generation plant **fault tree analysis** can be used to pinpoint likely failures and the many possible pathways through which they can be transmitted to other parts of the system. This is particularly important for systems where there is a possibility, however remote, of serious explosions, leaks, emissions or collapses – *e.g.* nuclear plants, chemical factories, large buildings, dams.

Other environmental processes may entail less dramatic accidents than those mentioned above, but it is equally important to identify the pathways through which they operate. For example, the potential contamination of groundwater by animal waste and agro-chemical residues, and by land-fill sites, will depend heavily on soil conditions, the geological sub-stratum, rainfall, the type and periodicity of discharges, etc. In this case the pathways of contamination are complex, and may need to be modelled by computer.

In another common case, soil erosion and sedimentation, the likelihood of erosion can be predicted using such models as the Universal Soil Loss Equation (Box 5.1). The movement of soil particles may also be predictable over short distances. But the deposition of soil downstream in rivers, irrigation channels, reservoirs and estuaries is often very difficult to predict and model, except for geographically small systems. Nevertheless, the first step in risk assessment is to understand the predisposing factors, the likely trigger events, and the pathways through which subsequent damage occurs.

Nevertheless, the first step in risk assessment is to understand the predisposing factors, the likely trigger events, and the pathways through which subsequent damage occurs.

ii) *Specifying the size and severity of the risk*

A risk has two properties – probability and magnitude. Before the question of probability is considered, the size of possible outcomes needs to be established.

For a particular plot, cultivation practices, and crop, the possible amount of soil erosion could, for instance, be expressed in terms of the loss of varying amounts of soil depth (in cm.) per year, depending on rainfall.

In the case of groundwater contamination – *e.g.* from landfill sites – one outcome may be the complete loss of the aquifer for human use once the presence of harmful elements exceeded critical levels. For flood risk estimation, the amount of damage to property associated with different flood severities (*e.g.* 1 in 100 year, 1 in 20 year event) can be specified.

In the case study later in this chapter, the potential effect of coastal water pollution on tourism is expressed in terms of the number of swimmers contracting gastroenteritis once the coliform level exceeds USEPA standards for swimmable water.

Certain environmental dangers have a low probability but an extremely high severity, *e.g.* collapse of a large dam, explosion at a chemical works, leak of radioactive material from a nuclear plant, a catastrophic flood, a water-related epidemic, etc. These are referred to as **zero-infinity** problems, and pose particular challenges to risk management, to which we revert below.

Evidence on the severity of possible environmental damage can be obtained from various sources – historical observation (*e.g.* flood damage), field trials and observations (*e.g.* soil erosion, acid rain), the transfer of dose-response relationships or functions established elsewhere, *e.g.* water pollution and the health of swimmers, modelling (*e.g.* groundwater contamination, nuclear plant safety), laboratory or control group trials (*e.g.* corrosion from air pollution), etc.

A crucial dimension of risk is the size of the **exposed population**, *e.g.* the number of people living near an environmental hazard, the number of swimmers in polluted waters, the number of people eating fish likely to be contaminated, etc.

For the purpose of economic analysis, the above information needs to be turned into economic values using the kind of techniques explained in earlier chapters of this book.

iii) Estimating probabilities and expected values

A probability measures the chance of a specified event happening. If it is based on scientific observation and estimation it is described as an **objective probability**, whereas if it is derived from judgements of professionals and decision-makers it is a **subjective probability**.

If different outcomes are mutually-exclusive, the sum of their probabilities is 1.0 (Box 9.3).

Where outcomes are not mutually-exclusive probabilities need not sum to 1.0. One way of expressing such probabilities is as a chance of x in a million of a particular event happening, based on historical records, epidemiological data, etc. If it can be shown that x people "normally" die from exposure to benzine fugitive emissions,

---

Box 9.3. **Calculation of expected values ($)**

Possible outcomes	Probability	Expected value
+5	0.3	1.5
0	0.3	0
−3	0.4	−1.2
	1.0	0.3

In the above table, a project has three possible outcomes, the first a positive benefit of 5, the second a benefit of zero, the third a loss of −3, their probabilities might be estimated to be, respectively, 0.3, 0.3 and 0.4 (totalling 1.0). If the size of each outcome is multiplied by its probability, and the three results summed, the result is the **expected value of the project**, which is 0.3 in the above example.

and y people from car accidents on unlit motorways, then these can be used as the probability of such events, assuming comparable circumstances.

Decision makers influenced solely by the objective expected value of the project would be interested in the fact that the probable outcome is a small benefit. However, as we shall see below, many decision-makers are not indifferent between the probability of a net gain and a significant chance of a loss. Expected values are useful where decision-makers and their constituents are risk-neutral. Where this is not the case, the analyst needs to take account of risk perception and subjective preferences, to which we now turn.

9.3. Risk Perception and Subjective Preferences

Most people are not risk-neutral, in other words interested only in objective expected values. Some are gamblers, and prefer risky situations, others are risk-averse. Some risks, although objectively very small, would be so catastrophic for the individuals or societies exposed to them that people are prepared to take extreme measures to reduce the risks still further.

Farmers are rational to be risk-averse in approaching a new crop or agronomic package, if the risk of failure would expose them to the loss of their land or crippling indebtedness. A business manager cannot afford to view profits and losses symmetrically if a loss would expose him/her to redundancy, prosecution or compromised career prospects. A politician would lose face, and perhaps office, from the failure of a public initiative. Many societies have taken their fear of major nuclear plant accidents – objectively very small – to the point where they oppose nuclear plant projects. As a general point, expert opinion and the public at large frequently differ on the relative importance of different hazards.

Expected value is supposedly the outcome objectively determined on the basis of weighted probability. Probabilities are determined by "expert" opinion or by the statistical analysis of past events. However, Acceptable Risk Analysis reminds us that many "objective" risks have a large judgemental component, especially for new and intricate hazards (Fishhoff *et al.*, 1981).

Environmental economics purports to use individual **preferences** as the basis of valuation. If people prefer a less risky outcome, even one with a lower expected value, this should be reflected in the analysis. Applying preferences to expected values produces **expected utility**. On this approach, the various outcomes should be weighted not only by their (objective) probability, but also by their respective utilities. In the example in Box 9.3, if the decision-maker were particularly averse to a loss an unusually high weight would be attached to this outcome. If a double weight were applied to the loss outcome, the overall expected value/utility of the project would fall to **minus** 0.9.

In practice, the production of expected utilities is an arbitrary process. Decision-makers, their constituents, and the general public perceive risks in very subjective ways, and react accordingly. In the next section we examine certain decision principles that allow for risk-averseness.

9.4. Dealing with Risk

The issue of uncertainty should if possible be turned into one of managing risk. This is a question of investing in information, which can take several forms, such as further research, setting up pilot projects, or delaying the project pending further reconnaissance.

Once the major possible outcomes are known, and probabilities attached to them, the views of the various parties whose interests are affected should be canvassed. This would determine the degree of risk-averseness amongst the stakeholders.

In the common situation where the parties concerned are risk-averse, the broad options are to redesign projects or to choose different ones.

Redesigning projects aims to eliminate or reduce those elements of risk that are of most concern. Sensitivity and switching value analysis should be used to identify variables of particular importance to the project. This information should be used in conjunction with data on the risk perceptions and preferences of the parties concerned. Projects can be modified or supplemented accordingly.

For instance, an afforestation project may be highly sensitive to the survival of young trees in the face of livestock depredations. In that case, it may be sensible to invest in more fencing or guards. An industrial project may pose risks of water contamination if its internal pollution control system fails; in this case investment in back-up facilities may be justified. In general, increasing spending on monitoring, inspection and enforcement could help to reduce environmental risk, though at the expense of higher recurrent costs.

The alternative is to devise **decision rules** that suit the preferences of decision makers and those they represent. Some of these are designed to mitigate the worst fears of decision-makers. For instance:

- **Minimax** is the principle of minimising the maximum loss expected from a project.
- **Maximin** maximises the minimum likely outcome.
- **Minimum regret** minimises the difference between the worst outcome and others. Regret measures the difference between the returns that could have been achieved and those that actually are achieved.

Applying these criteria will usually have a cost, compared to choosing the project or option with the highest (objective) expected value. Managing risk is not free, but yields some utility to those affected. The size of the trade-off between the sacrifice of (expected) returns and the avoidance of unwanted outcomes is something that can only be decided by the parties involved.

As an aid to such choices, analysts can construct **payoff matrices** and **regret matrices**. The Payoff Matrix depicts the outcomes associated with various choices (of projects or strategies) in each of the possible "states of nature". It may appear, for instance, that the project with the highest return under satisfactory rainfall is also that with the lowest return if rainfall is poor.

Risk-averse operators may opt for a project with a lower return under good rainfall conditions and a higher return for poor rainfall conditions. Choosing the latter option would entail a sacrifice (a regret) if rainfall turned out to be good. Conversely, if rainfall were poor, the former option would entail a regret. A Regret Matrix sets out the opportunity costs (regrets) of each choice.

A risk-neutral decision-maker would not proceed with the scheme. But someone who was extremely risk-averse would proceed, regarding the expected loss as insurance against the occurrence of the maximum loss. How much "insurance" it is worth spending in this case can be judged by the probabilities contained in the above table. The probability of the largest losses is actually very small – less than 1 per cent.

An alternative approach to these results is to calculate the cost of making the wrong decision. This can be either building it when it turns out not to be feasible, or not building it when it **would** have been feasible. This concept is the expected **opportunity loss**.

From information in the table the expected opportunity loss from building the project when it turns out not to be feasible is $17.5 million (the weighted probabilities in the top half of the table). On the other hand the opportunity loss from **not** building it when it turns out to be feasible is $5.8 million (the weighted probabilities in the lower half of the table).

Box 9.4. **Case Study: A Public Sewerage Project in the Caribbean**

This is the same project described in Chapter 6, which contains relevant background information. Certain important facts were lacking: data on the impact of sewage on the environment and human health; studies of the quality of coastal waters, which were incomplete and inconclusive; the wider causes of the observed decline in the fishing catch were not known; the relative contribution of other sources of pollution had not been investigated. For these reasons it was decided to use a range of values for both costs and benefits, with probability distributions for each.

For investment and operating costs normal probability distributions were used, the mean of which was the engineering estimates plus contingency allowance, with an 80 per cent confidence interval defined by a range 15 per cent above and 15 per cent below the central estimate. The four types of benefit were: the contingent valuation estimates of household benefits, both inside and outside the area to be connected up; fisheries benefits; coastal erosion benefits; and tourism benefits.

CV benefits were handled using a normal distribution that assumed an 80 per cent confidence interval within plus or minus 40 per cent of the central value. This wide range was considered to be justified in view of the possible errors and biases in the CV method.

Fisheries benefits were assessed on certain alternative scenarios, after taking local specialist advice. Without the project it was assumed that the fishery's yield would decline to zero after 10 years, and with the project yields would increase to 1980 levels in the ten years after project completion. Because the estimates rested solely on assumptions, a uniform distribution 50 per cent around the central estimate was used (*i.e.* any estimate within the range is equally likely).

The benefits from preventing **coastal erosion** were treated as potential savings in the cost of beach replacement (nourishment). The expectation was that cleaner coastal waters would encourage the formation of reefs and the growth of marine vegetation, both of which would help to stabilise beaches. The range of benefits was from no difference, to a reduction in the need for nourishment from once every 5 years to once every 20 years. These costs were annualised, and assigned a uniform probability distribution within the above range.

Handling **tourism benefits** proved to be the most complex part of the analysis. There were grounds for believing that, without the project, the percolation of untreated sewage and the disposal of septage into coastal waters would diminish the appeal of the water to swimmers and increase the risk of them contracting infectious diseases. There may even have been a risk of an outbreak of typhoid or cholera. These events would be likely to lead to a loss of tourism income, temporarily or even permanently.

However, assessing the size of these risks was hampered by poor information on the key links in the chain of reasoning, namely:

* the likelihood that coastal waters had reached a critical level of contamination;
* the effect of this on swimmers;
* the impact on tourism.

(continued on next page)

(continued)

Data on pollution was assessed against the USEPA standards for swimmable water, namely that the geometric mean for fecal coliforms should be less than 200 per 100 millilitres, and that the level of 400 coliforms per 100 litres in any 30-day period should be exceeded for no more than 10 per cent of the time. A specialist consultant survey had established that the waters currently fell within the EPA mean, and was not expected to exceed that mean until the year 2000.

Health risks to swimmers were assessed in the light of rather limited epidemiological data. In general, although swimming in water polluted by sewage may lead to hepatitis A, typhoid, shigellosis. cholera and gastroenteritis, a quantitative relationship has been established only with the last mentioned. The USEPA standard is consistent with 19 out of 1 000 swimmers contracting gastroenteritis. If the fecal coliform count increased from 200 to 800 per 100 millilitres, the incidence of gastroenteritis would increase 1.8 times.

In the absence of data on the current frequency with which water quality levels exceeded the EPA standard, scenarios were constructed based on the growing probability that critical levels would be exceeded in a particular year, provoking a public health "crisis". The response of tourism to the occurrence of a crisis was modelled by assuming that, without any public health problems, visitor days would grow by between 0.2 per cent and 2 per cent p.a. If a public health crisis did occur, it was assumed that visitation would decline permanently by between 0 per cent and 50 per cent. Declines of more than 20 per cent were assigned a 15 per cent probability, whereas declines of less than 20 per cent were given an 85 per cent rating. The economic value of this decline was calibrated from the estimated net foreign exchange value of tourism, taken to be $30-40 million p.a.

The analysis generated a large number of possible rates of return, calculated on a special computer programme. The results ranged from 0.8 per cent to 26.8 per cent, with a best estimate of 8.2 per cent. The expected NPV was minus US$11.7 million. Thus, the most likely outcome was a modest loss. If the project **were** implemented, the maximum loss would be $45 million, approximately the capital cost of the scheme. If it were **not** undertaken, the country would be exposed to a small risk of a loss of $127 million. The range of outcomes, and their probabilities, is set out in the Table below.

Probability of Losses and Gains if the Project is Undertaken
(dollar amounts are present value)

Possible loss (US$ millions)	Probability (per cent)
0-9	9
9-18	15
18-27	26
27-36	23
36-45	4
Probability project not feasible	78
Possible gains (US$ millions)	**Probability (per cent)**
0-25	11
25-51	7
51-76	1
76-102	0
102-127	0
Probability project feasible	21

The data can also be used to identify the **cost of uncertainty**, which in this case is the **regret** incurred when the best decision is made, namely to reject the project. If perfect foresight and information could be bought, it would be rational to pay up to $5.8 million for it. The analysis shows that the two areas where better information would be of greatest value were the contingent valuation estimates of benefits, and the likely effects on tourism. It was estimated that a study costing no more than $100 000 could have gone a long way to resolving whether individual beaches complied with EPA standards or not. This is very much less than the cost of uncertainty as defined above.

Points to note from the case study

- This is a sophisticated use of probability techniques to make uncertainty about key variables manageable for appraisal purposes. The probabilities are, with a few exceptions, given by standard statistical frequency distributions (normal or uniform). Computer programmes are used to generate the large number of possible outcomes.

- The cost of uncertainty is estimated as a useful check on the scale of spending that would be warranted on further studies. The actual cost of a further survey falls well within this figure.

- There is a small probability of a public health catastrophe. This is an example of a "zero-infinity" problem. The cost of avoiding this likelihood, which could be viewed as insurance, is illustrated.

- The notion of "regret" appears here as the opportunity loss from taking the wrong decision.

- Calibrating the link between water pollution and health was done from US evidence.

9.5. Conclusion

- The treatment of uncertainty and risk looms large in environmental appraisal. Converting uncertainty into risk is essential to make the problem tractable.

- Investing in information is one approach to reducing uncertainty. Delaying the project, setting up a pilot project, research or EIA are all options. However, the cost of getting information should be kept in mind – it should not be allowed to become an end in itself but should be commensurate with expected gains.

- Sensitivity analysis and switching values should be used to indicate the kind of outcomes of most significance to the project.

- Risk assessment begins by identifying the processes (pathways) involved, then assesses the size and probability of the various outcomes, and estimates their respective economic values.

- A project's expected value signifies its weighted probable outcome, but ignores the preferences for different outcomes held by people affected. Risk aversion is a common case.

- Risk aversion can be accommodated by investing in information, "designing out" problematic features, selecting decision rules that suit the decision-maker's preferences, and/or applying the Precautionary Principle. Managing risk in these ways usually has a cost, which should not be overlooked.

Further References and Sources

The project described in Box 9.5 is derived from the same source as that in Box 6.3 of Chapter 6, and is referred to at the end of Chapter 6.

Environmental risk assessment: dealing with uncertainty in Environmental Impact Assessment, Asian Development Bank, Environment Paper No. 7, Manila, 1990, is a useful and practical discussion of risk assessment methods, with guidelines.

The references in this chapter are as follows:

AHMAD: An appraisal of the Day Forest in Djibouti, in Munasinghe, Mohan (ed.), *Environmental economics and natural resource management*, World Bank/CIDIE. Washington, DC, 1993

FISCHHOFF, BARUCH, *et al.*, *Acceptable Risk*, Cambridge University Press, Cambridge, 1981.

Chapter 10

ENVIRONMENTAL PRICING

The Manual began (Chapter 1) with an account of the various ways in which decisions affecting the environment may be distorted by the use of market prices, made even worse in some cases by governments' actions. Market failures and policy distortions conspire to cause environmental degradation. The air pollution caused by a power station imposes costs on others (externalities): if these costs could be quantified and charged to the power utility, less pollution would be likely. Where this is encouraged by government subsidies to energy prices (oil and coal) this is a policy distortion which adds to environmental costs.

Much of this Manual has been about how this damage can be valued in economic terms. It is now time to examine how valuation can be put to work correcting market failures and policy distortions. If estimates can be made of the environmental costs (or benefits) of specific decisions, this furnishes governments with data useful for policy-making – raising taxes, prices or charges, granting subsidies, or other purposes.

Environmental pricing is useful in at least four contexts:

i) in performing cost-benefit analyses of projects and new regulations and policies. Where an Environmental Impact Assessment is required for these purposes, the inclusion of valuation can help to turn this into a cost-benefit analysis;

ii) environmental costing, where valuation can provide data useful for "green taxes" (*e.g.* proposed carbon taxes) and environmental "adders" (*e.g.* for electric power utilities);

iii) the production of environmental accounts which give a more accurate statement of national income, or the profits and losses of companies;

iv) in natural resource damage assessments, *e.g.* major pollution events.

In the USA cost-benefit analysis has to be carried out for all major regulations, including environmental ones (Executive Orders 12291 and 12866). Some

US electricity regulators insist on the quantification of the environmental damage caused by power stations ("electricity adders") and use these data in approving new investments and in sanctioning the "merit order" working of existing stations. This indicates the importance of using the valuation methods explained earlier in this Manual.

Another example of the potential role of valuation in environmental pricing is the use of damage estimates for carbon emissions through the Greenhouse Effect. These have been used as the basis of proposals for a Carbon Tax to be applied in countries of the European Union, to be levied per unit of the carbon content of different fuels. The same estimates have also been used, more controversially, to justify subsidies for afforestation in temperate countries, on the grounds that the growth of wood absorbs atmospheric carbon, avoiding the losses identified with global warming.

This chapter has two main parts:

- an account of the general principles applying to environmental pricing;

- a description of the policy levers available to governments in conducting environmental policy, illustrated by a discussion of environmental pricing in certain key areas.

10.1. Principles of Environmental Pricing

In environmental appraisal, prices have to be applied to various kinds of resources. These can be divided into three main types:

- resources that are directly consumed, for which **user charges** should be levied (*e.g.* energy, water, admittance to a game park);

- those that are indirectly used up, such as environmental 'sink' functions (*e.g.* capacity of the air and water to assimilate wastes). These should be subject to **emissions or waste charges**;

- an environmental resource which is embodied in a product (*e.g.* the energy content of a canned drink), for which a **product tax or charge** is appropriate.

Each of the above situations calls for a specific modification of the general approach. However, as a general principle, anyone using environmental resources or services should pay a price that reflects three distinct types of cost. In short:

The cost of using a natural resource comprises three elements:

- the direct cost of extraction, production or harvesting;
- any external, environmental, costs which this causes;
- the **user cost**, which is akin to a depletion cost, and represents the value of the future loss of output from consuming the resource now.

Economic valuation as discussed in this Manual can contribute by providing more accurate and more complete estimates of each of these cost elements.

Applied to a **finite resource**, such as natural gas, the price should, in principle, cover several cost elements:

- Firstly, the direct costs of extraction, which in the long term would have to include an allowance for the overhead of exploration, research and capital outlays.

- Secondly, any environmental externalities from the gas operations, such as chemical contamination of water, destruction of wetlands and wildlife, etc.

- Thirdly, the user cost representing the depletion of the resource. The size of this last item depends mainly on the expected length of life of the resource, and on the cost of the substitute (or "backstop" technology); strictly, it is the extra (discounted) cost per unit of output of replacing future production by substitutes or backstop technology. In one study of natural gas in Trinidad, the user cost was found to be quite small (7 per cent of extraction cost), reflecting the size of the reserve and hence the effect of heavy discounting of extra future costs.

In respect of **renewable resources**, such as agricultural land, forests, rivers, groundwater and the waste assimilation function of air or water, the same principle holds, though the concept of user cost does not automatically apply. Using a resource within its sustainable yield imposes no user cost, in the sense that no future output is sacrificed. Farming that does not cause long term erosion or nutrient depletion, fishing that falls within the safe maximum catch of the fishery, groundwater extraction which is less than the natural replenishment rate of the aquifer – these are all cases where present use is not at the expense of future consumption, and where user cost is zero.

Applying these principles to pricing irrigation water, for example, would entail:

- Firstly, charging the full economic cost of supply, including operation and maintenance (O & M), and an appropriate share of the capital costs of installing the offtake, storage and distribution works. A comprehensive measure of costs is given by the long run marginal cost (LRMC) of that particular water scheme, which is the total discounted cost of providing the next increment of capacity. At present, in most countries farmers receive water either free or at a price which barely covers O & M cost levels, and as a result water is often wasted, used on low-value crops, or applied excessively leading to the salinisation of the soil. To this should be added:

- Secondly, an element reflecting any environmental externalities. This could be the environmental costs of dams and reservoirs, the cost of water-related disease in irrigated areas (if that could be calculated) or even the benefit to adjacent groundwater users from leakage from unlined irrigation canals.

Complications

There are a number of complications entailed in applying the above pricing principle:

i) Renewable resources may be used at an unsustainable level, in other words in excess of their sustainable yield (SY). This begs the question whether the SY of these natural systems is meaningful and measurable, and experts differ on this point. However, that part of present consumption which is in excess of a resource's sustainable yield represents depletion, and is a user cost. Logging hardwood forests, without replanting with the species extracted, has a clear user cost. In this case the inherent value of the timber (its "stumpage value", or "economic rent") is a gift of nature which is taken without being replenished, and is at the expense of future forest users.

ii) Environmental costs of use should be distinguished from those of manufacture. One type of car engine might be very "green" in that it produces few emissions, but its manufacture might be highly polluting – and vice versa. If possible, the two effects should be tackled separately; emissions through differential petrol taxes, or taxes on the sales price of the car, and manufacturing through pollution charges. Sometimes, however, administrative considerations will dictate that one tax has to serve for both effects.

iii) "Life-cycle" impacts take account of the environmental implications of materials incorporated in the product, *e.g.* the environmental effects of steel, plastic and leather used in manufacturing a motor vehicle. One way of dealing with this point is to make sure that the cost of the materials and components at their own point of production incorporates environmental factors (*e.g.* materials that are particularly energy-intensive should be charged the full cost of energy, or pay the full pollution charge).

iv) One aspect of life-cycle costs is the expense of disposing of the product once it is used. This applies to paper, plastic and glass containers, but also to durable goods such as cars and batteries, and more seriously to heavy metals, hazardous waste, nuclear reactors and spent nuclear fuel. Packages and cars could be levied with a product charge to cover the social costs of their disposal. Alternatively, a refundable deposit could be included in their price, to be refunded when the user returned the item, or disposed of it in an approved place. As for defraying the costs of dismantling a dangerous factory or reactor, an operator, subject to the legal obligation of rendering the site safe after production ceases, would have an incentive to recover the final cost through the price of the product.

v) Implementing environmental pricing raises the theoretical problem of the **second best**. If distortions such as subsidies cause an environmental problem, the removal of these distortions is clearly desirable. But, in a highly distorted economy, removing one distortion may cause problems of its own, and may leave environmental pressures worse than before. To greatly simplify the principle, if it is not possible to achieve the 'best', namely removal of all distortions, then the removal of some of them does not necessarily improve the situation, and may make it worse.

One example would be the removal of a subsidy on commercial fuel, which had the effect of increasing the use of wood and charcoal in cooking and heating, leading to deforestation. In this case, other distortions remain (the failure to include user cost in the price of fuelwood, the high cost of fuel-efficient stoves, etc.) which would need to be simultaneously corrected. In general terms, the principle of the second best should force policy-makers to consider the design of minimum packages of measures, properly sequenced, with their potential side-effects taken care of.

10.2. Environmental Policy Levers

One basic choice facing governments implementing environmental policies is between the use of compulsion and regulation, on the one hand, and the manipulation of incentives, on the other. These alternative approaches have been dubbed **command and control** or **direct regulations**, on the one hand, and the use of **economic instruments**, on the other. The two types can be used in combination to tackle certain problems (indeed this "mixed approach" is applied in many instances).

There are other types of measures, such as the use of exhortation, persuasion, demonstration, appeal to the national good, etc. which do not fall into these two categories. There is also a large set of measures under the general headings of "reforming property rights" and "reducing transactions costs" which are basic to the success of specific environmental policies. These can be regarded as indirect, supporting actions, though are nonetheless important for that.

Projects and spending programmes are also part of the armoury of environmental policy: in some cases projects can substitute for policy measures (*e.g.* traffic management schemes for road pricing), in other cases they can complement each other (*e.g.* investments in cleaner public power stations alongside increases in electricity prices and pollution taxes).

There is a much wider group of economic policy actions which have environmental implications, and which can be manipulated for environmental gain even though this is not their prime purpose (*e.g.* components of structural adjustment programmes. The various ways of classifying environmental policy measures are illustrated in Box 10.1.

Environmental policy is often discussed as though there was a straight choice between command and control measures and economic instruments. As Box 10.1 indicates, the choice is much wider than that. Moreover, the four kinds of targeted

---

Box 10.1. **Types of Environmental Policy Measure**

	Examples
***i*) Targetted**	
Command and control	Air and water quality laws Waste disposal regulations
Economic instruments	Charges, taxes, subsidies, deposit refund systems, tradeable permits
Exhortation	Publicity, propaganda, "good practice" demonstrations
Projects and programmes	Afforestation, installation of cleaner technology
***ii*) Indirect and supportive**	
Property rights reforms	Land, leasehold tenure, rights of access, community control
Reduced transactions costs	Better information, simpler legal procedures, titling, legal reforms
***iii*) General economic measures**	Structural adjustment, exchange rate, budget, monetary policy, foreign investment code

---

Box 10.2. **Reforms in Energy Pricing**

If the price of oil and its products is fixed too low, it encourages over-depletion of reserves and air pollution through unbridled and wasteful use by vehicles, power stations and factories. The basic aim should be to raise the price of oil and its products. This could be done by raising prices directly (if the oil company is in public ownership, or subject to price control or regulation) or by imposing higher taxes on oil products (if it is private). The price increase could be timed to coincide with devaluation, which would raise the border value of oil (in domestic currency) and provide a separate rationale for the price change.

Parastatal reforms, affecting national oil and energy utilities, included in structural adjustment programmes, would also provide the motive and opportunity to overhaul national energy prices. All these measures are likely to be more effective if they are supported by a public information campaign for energy savings, in which subsidies for energy-efficient appliances and buildings might also feature. These policy measures might also be reinforced by spending on energy efficiency audits and rehabilitation programmes in utilities.

However, if reforms in the commercial energy sector are not to lead to the substitution of fuelwood for the higher-priced commercial product, at the expense of the forests, complementary measures will be needed to restore the relative price of fuelwood and charcoal compared to their commercial substitutes. Tighter controls over firewood cutting, and a reduction in the issue of wood-cutting licences may be effective (command and control measures). It is, however, notoriously difficult to "internalise" environmental and user costs in the price of fuelwood, and raising taxes and licence fees on wood merchants may cause them to increase their exploitation (to cover their higher fixed charges). It may be feasible to alter property rights, giving concessionaires a stake in the sustainable management of their areas, or restoring community control over local forests, or permitting greater private ownership of commercial forests.

---

measure often work best in combination, and in any case need to be fully backed up by indirect and supportive measures. In addition, the effect of targetted policies can easily be negated by general economic measures which tug incentives in contrary directions.

Box 10.2 illustrates the range of policies available in the case of energy pricing.

The following section discusses command and control measures, economic instruments, and general economic measures – all key policies in the context of environmental pricing.

Command and Control (C & C) measures

C & C aims to influence environmental behaviour by regulation and prohibition. Certain practices may be banned by law (*e.g.* tipping radioactive waste into public drains, exporting ivory), while other activities may be subject to ceilings or discretionary permits (*e.g.* release of wastewater into rivers or lakes, hunting whale and game animals). Physical planning, land use zoning and building permits are also attempts to preserve local amenity and environmental quality. Some regulations are based on the impact of pollution on a receptor (*e.g.* control of the release of particulate matter according to the preservation of minimum air quality in a specific air quality "basin"; others attempt to control emissions by banning certain production processes and types of equipment, while allowing others.

There are thus many types of C & C measures, and some of them have financial penalties built in (*e.g.* the use of fines to ensure compliance, and the use of licence fees typically to cover the costs of administration). If they are implemented as intended, C & C measures are categorical, and leave members of the public with no choice but to comply with publicly-stated standards of environmental quality. Where, on the other hand, laws and regulations are poorly enforced and commonly flouted, and fines and penalties too small to be punitive, a potential offender will be tempted to judge the risk (and cost) of prosecution against the cost of compliance. In this situation, a C & C measure is more like an economic incentive, in which the decision is taken by balancing private costs and benefits.

C & C measures do not operate **directly** on prices. However, they still have a potential role in environmental pricing:

- They affect costs and benefits indirectly. If producers or householders are banned from their preferred behaviour, their alternatives will normally be more costly, or have fewer benefits. For instance, producers disallowed from discharging untreated effluent into a river have to incur the expense of treating it, or altering their production process, or disposing of it elsewhere.

- They can provide 'fail safe' limits within which economic instruments can work. For example, a pollution tax proportional to the amount and/or concentration of pollutant could be backstopped by an absolute prohibition on certain kinds of pollution (*e.g.* heavy metals) or pollutants in excess of a certain concentration.

- The apparatus of C & C (environmental quality standards, performance monitoring, and enforcement systems) is a pre-requisite of certain market-based solutions. The concept of tradeable permits for air pollution control (see below) depends on a highly developed system for setting local air quality standards, monitoring air quality, inspecting factories and premises, and enforcement through fines and other penalties.

Surveys of environmental policy instruments in OECD countries reveals that C & C is still the predominant approach, though the use of economic instruments has made some recent gains. (OECD, 1994*a*). This broad picture is even more true in economies in transition and developing countries.

The shortcomings of C & C are the same as the advantages of economic instruments, to which we now turn.

Economic Instruments (EIs)

The essential purpose of EIs is to persuade people and firms to adopt environmentally-friendly behaviour by changing their economic incentives to do so. Unlike C & C measures, EIs allow an element of choice, and operate directly on costs and prices.

The principal categories of EIs are the following (OECD, 1994*a*):

Charges and taxes, intended to penalise anti-social practices and the use of certain products, justified by the Polluter Pays Principle. They directly raise costs of the offending party, producing an incentive to reduce or cease the practice concerned. In most cases they will raise revenue, unless the charges/taxes discourage use entirely. Charges refer to the *quid pro quo* for the provision of a service (*e.g.* public treatment of effluent), whereas taxes are an unrequited levy, though the distinction is not always possible to uphold.

There are many examples, including effluent charges, product charges (*e.g.* on harmful substances), and differential taxes (*e.g.* on leaded and unleaded petrol, or according to the size of vehicle engine). Outside the realm of pollution, charges and taxes could apply to license fees for hunting or fishing, entry to nature reserves, levies on the growth of crops considered to be erosive, taxes on pesticide, etc.

Subsidies are the reverse of taxes and charges, and are aimed at promoting the consumption of environmentally-friendly products and services. Examples include subsidies on commercial heating and cooking fuels, where the alternative is charcoal and woodfuel, the subsidy to non-conventional power generation (wind), subsidies to fertiliser to discourage extensive modes of cultivation, etc. Subsidies have the disadvantage that they absorb public revenues, and are notoriously prone to be diverted and abused. Subsidies also offend the principle of the Polluter Pays.

Deposit refund schemes encourage users or producers of a potentially polluting good to dispose of the item safely. They work by imposing a surcharge on the price of the item, which is refunded when it is returned or safely disposed of. Deposit refund schemes are widespread for metal cans, glass bottles and plastic containers, and there are a few examples for fluorescent light bulbs, vehicle batteries and motor vehicle hulks (OECD, 1994a). Some of these schemes were introduced by producers for their own commercial reasons, while others have been promoted by governments for environmental reasons.

Market Creation (MC) entails trading the right to pollute (hence "tradeable permits"). In situations where pollution of air and water is subject to an upper limit, individual polluters may be allowed to buy and sell emissions "quotas". Where MC schemes exist, firms who introduce more efficient or less polluting processes economise on their original "quotas" and are free to sell them to other firms who cannot manage on their own quotas (e.g. those with old plant who are expanding output, or to new firms entering the area for the first time).

MC shares a number of advantages with pollution taxes, namely:

- They reward firms (and public utilities) that make their processes less polluting. and provide a continuing disincentive to polluting firms.

- They provide a continuous spur to the search for pollution-saving. Unlike C & C methods, which usually provide a once-for-all motive to change production methods or equipment, MC is a dynamic process. Under MC, Firms needing quotas are forced into the market all the time, and even "clean" producers have an incentive to reduce their pollution to zero, since each unit of pollution has an opportunity cost (namely, what they could earn by selling the quota). Under pollution taxes, the same effect is produced by the continuing spur to minimise taxes. Both methods are 'technology forcing', providing a continuous motive for pollution reduction.

- They are more flexible than C & C: a polluting firm can continue its operations, but at a cost penalty.

- Both MC and pollution taxes encourage pollution abatement to be carried out by firms that can do it most efficiently, and who are then rewarded for it. C & C forces all firms to comply with the set standards, whatever their age, size or technological endowment. Some firms may only be able to comply at high cost, and some might be forced to close. In theory, under MC a given desired amount of pollution abatement is achieved at least total cost.

- Both methods can be used to generate public revenue. In the case of MC, the initial allocation of pollution quotas can be auctioned or sold to bidders (the alternative being to award quotas on the basis of present or historical emissions – 'grandfathering').

MC has the advantage over pollution taxes that, if properly monitored, a ceiling is placed on total emissions. With taxes, the total amount of emissions which result depends on the decisions of firms, comparing the cost of abatement with the benefits (avoided taxes). Emissions standards can also be made more stringent over time, which redoubles the incentive for participants to curb their emissions. It is also possible for environmental groups to buy quotas which they do not intend to use, thus tightening the pressure on remaining polluters.

The criticism that MC gives firms a "licence to pollute" is misconceived. MC can only work in a situation where pollution standards are in place and emissions from individual firms can be monitored and enforced. Emissions trading is a way of making the enforcement of standards more efficient and is compatible with any level of pollution desired by society.

In a wider sense, MC can describe any attempt to exchange environmental obligations or needs through market processes. There are cases of US electric power companies fulfilling their responsibilities to reduce greenhouse gas emissions, not by modifying their own processes but by investing in afforestation in Central America. Urban authorities in the Western States of the USA are buying water rights from farmers as a (cheaper) alternative to investing in their own supply sources. Under the US Wetland Mitigation Banking programme investors receive credit for the creation and enhancement of wetlands, which can be sold to developers modifying other wetland areas. There are also a few cases of tradeable rights in water pollution.

However, tradeable permits have made most headway in air pollution, especially in the USA. Since 1982 firms have been allowed Emission Reduction Credits (ERCs) for surplus emissions reductions achieved beyond baseline levels. These ERCs can be sold to other firms, saved for future use (banking), or used to offset emissions from other parts of the same industrial unit (netting). In practice, the overwhelming majority of trades have occurred within companies through the netting procedure. The other schemes that have been introduced cover inter-refinery trading of lead credits, and trading in sulphur dioxide emissions.

General economic measures

The policy measures discussed so far have all had the specific intention of benefiting the environment. But environmental policy-makers have a much wider variety of measures at their disposal, once they recognise the potential impact of general economic policies.

A number of the major macroeconomic policy devices available to governments have potentially important effects on the environment. Very often these will overwhelm the impact of more specific measures at the project or sector level. In every case they are likely to affect a far larger number of environmental users than can be reached by specific projects or targetted measures. Boxes 10.3 and 10.4 illustrate their scope.

Structural (and Sectoral) Adjustment Programmes (SAPs)

The opportunity to make simultaneous economic and institutional reforms arises in the course of SAPs carried out with the support of the World Bank and other donors. Hence the impact of SAPs on the environment has aroused widespread interest (e.g. Reed, 1992).

SAPs have three main purposes:

- to provide the financial resources for coping with debt servicing and balance of payments deficits over the medium term;

Box 10.3. **Environmental Impact of General Economic Measures**

Type of measure	Potential impact
Monetary policy	Interest and discount rates. Natural resources as inflationary hedges.
Fiscal stance	Taxes on resource use. Spending on green programmes. Reduced subsidies.
Exchange rate	Tree crops vs annuals. Protection for polluting industry.
Foreign investment codes	Attraction of polluting industry. Responsible behaviour by investors.
Capital market	Credit for resource management, pollution control.
Energy policy	Use of fuelwood, fossil fuel. Deforestation, air pollution.

Box 10.4.   **Industrial Policy and the Environment**

In a study of Egypt, ex-Yugoslavia, Algeria and Turkey it was found that the influence of general industrial policies predominated over specific anti-pollution measures. Subsidies for inputs like water, energy and other raw materials aggravated pollution of the Mediterranean. Controls over the prices of output (*e.g.* cement, fertiliser and chemicals) discouraged product recovery and recycling. The poor financial position of state enterprises made it difficult for them to finance resource recovery and investment in pollution abatement. The absence of incentives for good performance blunted the motive for the efficient use of inputs. In three of the countries negative real interest rates encouraged capital-intensive projects, which happened to be heavy polluters.

Source: Kosmo, 1989.

- to produce macroeconomic adjustment, by bringing aggregate demand into better balance with supply, in order to provide the conditions for non-inflationary growth; and

- to improve supply-side performance by removing distortions in specific markets, especially foreign exchange, energy, public utilities and agriculture.

SAPs are normally carried out alongside IMF stabilisation programmes focussing on the exchange rate, monetary policy and the budget.

The various policy conditions of an SAP can be related to each of its main objectives. In trade policy, common measures include the removal of import quotas, the reduction of tariffs, and improved export incentives. The aim of resource mobilisation is most frequently served by fiscal and budgetary reforms, the greater use of interest rates in allocating capital and credit, better control over external borrowing, and improvements in the finances of public enterprises.

Supply side objectives are typically served by the more efficient use of resources through: revised priorities in public investment; changes in agricultural prices; reduced scope for state marketing boards; reduced farm input subsidies; revision in energy prices and promotion of energy conservation; and an overhaul of industrial incentives. Finally, institutional reform typically includes measures to improve the design and implementation of public investment and support for the productive sectors. Reforms in the bureaucracy and privatisation may form a part of this sub-set of measures.

It is only recently that the potential impact of SAPs on the environment has become appreciated. Once the effects are understood, then the possibility arises of mitigating their negative impacts and capitalising on their positive aspects. The possibility of the same reform having both economic and environmental benefits has given rise to the notion of "win-win" policies (World Bank, 1992). However, there is still little experience of designing an SAP with positive environmental features, or with minimal environmental disturbance.

10.3. Conclusion

This final chapter has aimed to provide the link between economic valuation and decisions on environmental policy. The techniques discussed in Chapters 5, 6 and 7 can be used to produce quantified estimates of environmental impacts which can help to inform policymakers faced with decisions about taxes, charges, subsidies, etc. This chapter reviewed the range of measures that could serve as vehicles for environmental pricing. Although environmental values are useful shadow prices to use in appraisal and policy review, the real test of their utility comes when they are "internalised" in actual prices.

Further References and Sources

KOSMO, M., *Economic incentives and industrial pollution in developing countries*, paper produced for World Bank's Environment Department, July 1989.

OECD (1994) contains (Part V) a discussion of the principles underlying environmental pricing and policy, with many examples.

OECD (1994a), *Managing the environment: the role of economic instruments*, Paris (written by Opschoor, de Savornin Lohman and Vos), this is a comprehensive and detailed survey of the present use of economic instruments in OECD countries.

OECD (1993), *Economic instruments for environmental management in developing countries*, Paris, examines policy formation in the specific context of developing countries.

OECD (1995), *Environmental Taxes in OECD Countries*.

OECD (forthcoming), *Implementation Strategies for Environmental Taxes*.

PANAYOTOU (1993), is an introduction to the economics of environmental policy, focussing on the correction of market and policy failures.

PANAYOTOU, T., *Economic instruments for environmental management and sustainable development*, a paper prepared for the UN Environment Programme, 1994, provides an up-to-date and systematic analysis of the range of measures in operation, both for developed and developing countries.

WINPENNY (1991, Chapter 6) contains a review of the various environmental policy measures open to developing countries, with many examples.

WORLD BANK, *Economywide policies and the environment: emerging lessons of experience*, Washington, DC, 1994.

Appendix

A SHORT BIBLIOGRAPHY

The following is a consolidated list of the general books and key articles and papers referred to in the text. The more specialised items are omitted.

ABELSON, P., *Project appraisal and valuation methods for the environment, with special reference to developing countries,* to be published by Macmillan, London, 1995.

ASIAN DEVELOPMENT BANK, *Environmental risk assessment: dealing with uncertainty in Environmental Impact Assessment,* ADB Environment Paper No. 7, Manila, 1990.

BARDE, J.P., *Économie et politique de l'environnement,* Presses Universitaires de France, Paris, 1992.

BARDE, J.P. and PEARCE, D.W., *Valuing the environment. Six case studies,* Earthscan, London, 1991.

BOJO, J., MALER, K.G. and UNEMO, L., *Environment and development: an economic approach,* Kluwer, Dordrecht, 1990, new edition 1993.

BRADEN, J.B. and KOLSTAD, C.D. (ed.), *Measuring the demand for environmental quality,* Elsevier Science Publishers B.V., North Holland, Amsterdam, 1991.

BRIDGER, G.A. and WINPENNY, J.T., *Planning development projects: a practical guide to the choice and appraisal of public sector investments,* Her Majesty's Stationery Office (HMSO), London, 1983, new edition 1987.

DESAIGUES, B. and POINT, P., *Économie du patrimoine naturel, la valorisation des bénéfices de protection de l'environnement,* Economica, Paris, 1993.

DIXON, J.A., SCURA, L.F., CARPENTER, R.A. and SHERMAN, P.B., *Economic analysis of environmental impacts,* Earthscan, London, new edition 1994.

DIXON, J., JAMES, D. and SHERMAN, P.,(ed.), *Dryland management, Economic case studies,* Earthscan, London, 1990.

DIXON, J. and HUFSCHMIDT, M. (ed.), *Economic valuation techniques for the environment: a case study workbook,* Johns Hopkins, 1986.

FREEMAN, A.M. III, *The measurement of environmental and resource values: theory and methods,* Resources for the Future, 1993.

HUFSCHMIDT, M.M., JAMES, D.E., MEISTER, A.D., BOWER, B. and DIXON, J.A., *Environment, natural systems and development: an economic valuation guide,* Johns Hopkins, 1983.

INTERNATIONAL INSTITUTE FOR ENVIRONMENT and DEVELOPMENT (IIED)/WRI/IUCN, Directory of country environmental studies, London, 1993.

KOSMO, M., *Economic incentives and industrial pollution in developing countries,* Paper produced for World Bank's Environment Department, July 1989.

MARKANDYA, A. and PEARCE, D., *Environmental considerations and the choice of the discount rate in developing countries",* World Bank Environment Department Working Paper No. 9, Washington DC, 1988.

MITCHELL, R.C. and CARSON, R.T., *Using surveys to value public goods; the contingent valuation method,* Resources for the Future, Washington DC., 1989.

MUNASINGHE, M. (ed.), *Environmental economics and natural resource management in developing countries,* World Bank/CIDIE, Washington DC, 1993.

MUNASINGHE, M., *Environmental economics and valuation in development decisionmaking,* World Bank Environment Working Paper No. 51, 1992.

NAVRUD, S. (ed.), *Pricing the European Environment,* Scandinavian University Press/Oxford University Press, Oslo/Oxford/New York.

OATES, W.E. and CROPPER, M.L., "Environmental economics: a survey", *Journal of Economic Literature,* XXX, June 1992.

OECD, *Project and policy appraisal: integrating economics and environment* (Paris, 1994), written by Pearce, Whittington, Georgiou and James.

OECD, *Environmental Data* (regular), Paris.

OECD, *Environmental indicators: OECD core set,* Paris, 1994.

OECD (1994a), *Managing the environment: the role of economic instruments*, Paris (written by OPSCHOOR, DE SAVORNIN LOHMAN and VOS).

OECD (1993), *Economic instruments for environmental management in developing countries*, Paris.

OECD (Forthcoming), *Implementation Strategies for Environmental Taxes*. Paris.

OVERSEAS DEVELOPMENT ADMINISTRATION, *Manual of Environmental Appraisal*, London, 1992.

PANAYOTOU, T., *Economic instruments for environmental management and sustainable development*, a paper prepared for the UN Environment Programme, 1994, Nairobi.

PANAYOTOU, T., *Green markets*, Harvard Institute for International Development/International Center for Economic Growth and published by the Institute for Contemporary Studies, California, 1993.

PEARCE, D and TURNER, R.K., *Economics of natural resources and the environment*, Harvester Wheatsheaf, UK, 1990.

PEARCE, D., MARKANDYA, A. and BARBIER, E., *Blueprint for a green economy*, Earthscan, London, 1989.

PEARCE, D and MARKANDYA, A., *Environmental policy benefits: monetary valuation*, OECD, Paris, 1989.

UN DEVELOPMENT PROGRAMME (UNDP), *Human Development Report* (annual), New York.

UN ECONOMIC COMMISSION FOR EUROPE (UNECE), *The environment in Europe and North America* (annual), Geneva.

UN ENVIRONMENT PROGRAMME (UNEP), *Environmental Data Report* (regular), Nairobi.

WINPENNY, J.T., *Values for the environment: a guide to economic appraisal*, HMSO, London, 1991.

WORLD BANK, *Economywide policies and the environment: emerging lessons from experience*, Washington, DC, 1994.

WORLD BANK, *Environmental Assessment Sourcebook*, (3 volumes), Washington, DC, 1991.

WORLD RESOURCES INSTITUTE/UNDP/UNEP, *World Resources* (annual), Washington, DC.

WORLD BANK, *World Development Report* (annual), Washington, DC.

ECONOMIC DEVELOPMENT INSTITUTE (EDI)

The Economic Development Institute (EDI) of the World Bank invests in people and ideas as the most powerful means of development. It helps the World Bank and its member countries achieve the goals of sustainable and equitable development through strengthening national capacities to design and implement development policies and programs. To this end, EDI facilitates a learning dialogue on development through structured exchanges of ideas and experience among people. The EDI works with partner institutions to design and deliver courses and seminars and publishes high quality materials in support of those training activities.

OVERSEAS DEVELOPMENT INSTITUTE (ODI)

The Overseas Development Institute was founded in 1960 as an independent non-governmental centre for development research and a forum for discussion of the problems facing developing countries. The Institute is engaged in policy-related research on a wide range of issues which affect economic relations between the North and the South and which influence social and economic policies within developing countries. ODI maintains five specialist networks of practitioners and researchers in Relief and Rehabilitation, Agricultural Research and Extension, Water Resource Management, Pastoral Development, and Rural Development Foresty.

OECD PUBLICATIONS, 2, rue André-Pascal, 75775 PARIS CEDEX 16
PRINTED IN FRANCE
(97 1995 11 1) ISBN 92-64-14583-4 – No. 48225 1995